P9-CJN-457

Praise for *James Joyce: A Life*
by Edna O'Brien

"O'Brien's triumph is that while celebrating Joyce and his ecstatic quest to lay image on counterimage . . . she has drawn the desperation and sadness of the man whose name means joy."
—*The New York Times Book Review*

"Utterly engaging. O'Brien paints a portrait of the artist so vivid that he fairly leaps from these pages."
—*New York Daily News*

"Vivid . . . Elegantly captures both the brilliance and the sadness of a life given to the pursuit of literary beauty."
—*Utne Reader*

"Inspired."
—*Elle*

A LIPPER™ / PENGUIN BOOK

JAMES JOYCE

Edna O'Brien is the author of numerous books, including *The Country Girls Trilogy*, *The Light of the Evening*, *Byron in Love*, and *House of Splendid Isolation*. She is the recipient of the James Joyce Ulysses Medal. She lives in London, England.

EDNA O'BRIEN

James Joyce

—————

A Life

A LIPPER™ / PENGUIN BOOK

PENGUIN BOOKS

Published by the Penguin Group
Penguin Group (USA) Inc., 375 Hudson Street, New York, New York 10014, U.S.A.
Penguin Group (Canada), 90 Eglinton Avenue East, Suite 700, Toronto,
Ontario, Canada M4P 2Y3 (a division of Pearson Penguin Canada Inc.)
Penguin Books Ltd, 80 Strand, London WC2R 0RL, England
Penguin Ireland, 25 St Stephen's Green, Dublin 2, Ireland (a division of Penguin Books Ltd)
Penguin Group (Australia), 250 Camberwell Road, Camberwell,
Victoria 3124, Australia (a division of Pearson Australia Group Pty Ltd)
Penguin Books India Pvt Ltd, 11 Community Centre,
Panchsheel Park, New Delhi – 110 017, India
Penguin Group (NZ), 67 Apollo Drive, Rosedale, Auckland 0632,
New Zealand (a division of Pearson New Zealand Ltd)
Penguin Books (South Africa) (Pty) Ltd, 24 Sturdee Avenue,
Rosebank, Johannesburg 2196, South Africa

Penguin Books Ltd, Registered Offices:
80 Strand, London WC2R 0RL, England

First published in Great Britain by Widenfeld & Nicolson 1999
Published in the United States of America by Viking Penguin,
a member of Penguin Putnam Inc. 1999
Published in Penguin Books 2011

1 3 5 7 9 10 8 6 4 2

THE LIBRARY OF CONGRESS HAS CATALOGED THE HARDCOVER EDITION AS FOLLOWS:
O'Brien, Edna.
James Joyce / Edna O'Brien.
p.   cm. — (Penguin lives series)
"A Lipper / Viking book."
ISBN 0-670-88230-5 (hc.)
ISBN 978-0-14-311993-7 (pbk.)
1. Joyce, James, 1882–1941.   2. Novelists, Irish—20th century—Biography.
I. Title.   II. Series.
PR6019.09Z766   999
823'.912—dc21
[B]   99-23214

Printed in the United States of America
Designed by Francesca Belanger

Whack folthe dah, dance to your partner
Welt the flure, your trotters shake,
Wasn't it the truth I told you,
Lots of fun at Finnegan's Wake.

Irish Song

Contents

Contents

James Joyce

Once Upon a Time

ONCE UPON A TIME there was a man coming down a road in Dublin and he gave himself the name of Dedalus the sorcerer, constructor of labyrinths and maker of wings for Icarus who flew so close to the sun that he fell, as the apostolic Dubliner James Joyce would fall deep into a world of words—from the "epiphanies" of youth to the epistomadologies of later years.

James Joyce, poor joist, a funnominal man, supporting a gay house in a slum of despond. His name derived from the Latin and meant joy but at times he thought himself otherwise—a jejune Jesuit spurning Christ's terrene body, a lecher, a Christian brother in luxuriousness, a Joyce of all trades, a bullock-befriending bard, a peerless mummer, a priestified kinchite, a quill-frocked friar, a timoneer, a pool-beg flasher and a man with the gift of the Irish majuscule script.

A man of profligate tastes and blatant inconsistencies, afraid of dogs and thunder yet able to strike fear and subordination into those he met; a man who at thirty-nine would weep because of not having had a large family of his own yet cursed the society and the Church for whom his mother like so many Irish mothers was a "cracked vessel for childbearing." In all she bore sixteen children; some died in infancy, others in their early years, leaving her and her husband with a family of ten to provide for.

"Those haunted inkpots" Joyce called his childhood homes, the twelve or thirteen addresses as their financial fates took a tumble. First there was relative comfort and even traces of semi-grandeur. His mother, Miss May Murray, daughter of a Dublin wine merchant, versed in singing, dancing, deportment and politeness, was a deeply religious girl and a lifelong member of the Sodality of Our Lady. She was a singer in the church choir where her future and Rabelaisian husband John, ten years her senior, took a shine to her and set about courting her. His mother objected, regarding the Murrays as being of a lower order, but he was determined in his suit and even moved to the same street so as to be able to take her for walks. Courtships in Dublin were just that, through the foggy streets under the yellowed lamps, along the canal or out to the seashore which James Joyce was to immortalize in his prose—"Cold light on sea, on sand on boulders" and the speech of water slipping and slopping in the cups of rock. His father and mother had walked where he would walk as a young man, drifter and dreamer, who would in his fiction delineate each footstep, each bird call, each oval of sand wet or dry, the seaweed emerald and olive, set them down in a mirage of language that was at once real and transubstantiating and would forever be known as Joyce's Dublin. His pride in this was such that he said if the Dublin of his time were to be destroyed it could be reconstructed from his works.

James Augustine Joyce was their second son, born February 2, 1882. An infant, John, had died at birth, causing John Joyce to indulge in a bit of bathos, saying, "My life was buried with him." May Joyce said nothing; deference to her husband was native to her, that and a fatality about life's vicissitudes. John Joyce's life was not buried with his first son; he was a lively, lusty man and for many years his spirit and his humor prevailed. But sixteen pregnancies later, and almost as many house moves, impecunity, disappointments and children's deaths did make for a broken household. His enmity toward his wife's family and sometimes toward his wife herself was vented at all hours—the name Murray stank in his nostrils whereas the name Joyce imparted "a perfumed tipsy sensation." Only the Joyce ancestry appeared in photographs and the Joyce coat of arms was on proud display. He was a gifted man, a great tenor, a great raconteur and one whose wit masked a desperate savagery.

James, when young, was known as "Sunny Jim" and being a favorite he would steal out of the nursery and come down the stairs shouting gleefully, "I'm here, I'm here." By the time he was five he was singing at their Sunday musical parties and ac-companying his parents to recitals in the Bray Boat Club. By then too he was wearing glasses because of being nearsighted. That he loved his mother then is abundantly clear, identifying her with the Virgin Mary, steeped as he was in the ritual and precepts of the Catholic Church. She was such a pious woman that she trusted her confessor more than any member of her own family. She was possessive of Sunny Jim, warning him not to mix with rough boys and even disapproving of a valentine note which a young girl, Eileen Vance, had sent to him when he was six:

O Jimmie Joyce you are my darling
You are my looking glass from night till morning

I'd rather have you without one farthing
Than Harry Newall and his ass and garden.

His mother with her "nicer smell than his father" was the object of his accumuled tenderness and when he was parting from her he pretended not to see the tears under her veil.

Jesuits

THE GRIM STONE Castle of Clongowes Wood College was where he was enrolled at the age of "half past six." His father wanting the finest education for his little prodigy sent him to the Jesuits, where older boys "ragged" him as to whether he had kissed his mother before he fell asleep. Admitting to it, he saw his mistake and henceforth denied it. The Jesuits he called in his adult life a "heartless order that bears the name of Jesus by antiphrasis." Yet his indoctrination from them he thought invaluable. A photograph the day he left home shows James in Little Lord Fauntleroy outfit, kneeling by his mother, who was flanked by her husband and her father, two men inimicable to one another, John Joyce calling the father "the old fornicator" because he had been married twice and the father observing his quiet daughter becoming worn down with a pregnancy each year, infants to nurse and siblings to take care of.

Soon the reports were that James spent more time in the infirmary than in the classroom and to make his yearning all the worse he suffered an injustice which he never forgot and never forgave. Forgiveness was anathema to him. A boy had snatched his glasses and stood on them but a priest believed that Joyce had done it himself to avoid lessons and gave him a "pandying." He did not show his tears in public but at night he wept, fearing that he would die before his mother came to get him. He wrote a hymn to the two mothers, the earthly and the celestial one. As an altar boy, the ritual and liturgy of the Catholic Church engendered a kind of ecstasy in him and the Virgin Mother in her tower of ivory was the creature he adored. Church had all the pageantry of theater until he became aware of the scarifying sermons which inhuman prelates boomed out, gloating in their versions of punishment and their seething visions of hell. He absorbed it all, remembered it all and transcribed it into the languid and lacerating autobiographical novel *A Portrait of the Artist as a Young Man*. But the fear was so ingrained in him that he used to envisage death creeping from his extremities, in the same way as Socrates had observed the flow of the hemlock, the bright centers of the brain extinguished one by one, just like lamps, the soul's confrontation with God and then the designation for all time—heaven, purgatory or hell.

His stay there lasted just over three years and he left abruptly through lack of funds. So it was home to an even smaller house, where for months he tutored himself, wrote poetry and began a novel which has vanished without trace; the stint with the Christian Brothers and then to Belvedere College, another Jesuit school—"a Jesuit for life, a Jesuit for diplomacy" as he put it. But already from the mother he so loved he was distancing himself. When making his confirmation at Clongowes and being allowed to choose a saint's name he chose Aloysius, the saint who, in imitation of Pascal, would not allow his mother to embrace him because he feared contact with women. In his new school James excelled at lessons and won prizes for the best English compositions. The money helped to buy clothes and food for the needy family and even allowed for little trips to the theater. It was supposed that he would be a priest; so devout was he that he would stay on after Mass to have his private deliberations with God. His mother would boil rice especially for him because of his studiousness. When the family went picnicking to Howth or the Bull Wall at Clontarf he would bring little notebooks with summaries of history or literature, lists of French and Latin words, and while the other children swam he would set himself tests and get his mother to examine him. The priests who taught him recognized that he had a plethora of ideas in his head, one priest predicting that "Gussie" would be a writer.

The transition he underwent in just a few years has all the determination of a Samurai. He went from childlike tenderness to a scathing indifference, from craven piety to doubt and rebellion. His first sexual arousal happened when he was twelve and walking home with a young nurse who told him to turn away while she urinated. The sound of this was an excitement to him. A year later he was stopped by a prostitute and the wavering faith was soon to be quenched forever as he realized that he could not lead a life of sinlessness or celibacy. First it was covert, his life at home and at school one thing, his inner life quite another as he began to question the tenets of Church and family. Before long he went to the brothels and a fascination for these forbidden houses remained with him all his life. He viewed them to be the most interesting places in any city. He wrote about them in *Ulysses* and endowed them with a thrilling hallucinatory life that was hardly true of the seedy dungeons which he frequented. The girls he had met earlier, those vestals with whom he had played charades at Christmas parties, were prim and hypocritical—no match for one who had determined "to sin with another who would exult with him in that sin."

The Jesuits began to notice this laxity and questioned

Stanislaus whose role in life was that of a beleaguered younger brother, "as useful as an umbrella." Unnerved by their questioning of him, Stanislaus let it slip that James had a habit of romping in the bedroom with a young maid and so Mrs. Joyce was summoned. She dismissed the maid and warned the neighbors of the girl's transgression. Chastity at all costs and this in a house with only three bedrooms, eight or nine children, further conceivings and a father who came home drunk, irate and boisterous. "Bridebed, childbed, bed of death, ghostcandled"—the young James was witness to it all.

After the death of yet another child, Frederick, the desperate father tried to strangle the mother, seized her by the throat, shouting, "Now by God is the time to finish it." As bedlam broke out, with younger children in terror, James knocked his father to the floor and pinioned him there while his mother escaped to a neighbor's house. A few days later a police sergeant called to give the father a severe talking-to and while the beatings might have stopped, the threats and the shouting went on. For John Joyce, finding no outlets for his wayward gifts, his frustration had to be vented on his family. Walking across Capel Street Bridge half drunk one night, escorted by the young James, he decided that the boy needed a formative experience and held him upside down in the Liffey for several minutes. Yet no wrong done by that father wrankled because they were both "sinners."

Inkpots

OVER THE YEARS they moved to less and less salubrious districts, from south Dublin with its semblance of respectability, to the seaside at Bray, then back to Dublin to a small terraced house and then to humbler abodes on the north side of the city; near slums with cracked fanlights in the doorways and women in the nearby streets behind their barrows selling cabbages and potatoes. As they pitched tent in different quarters James drew a skeleton map of the city in his mind, his father predicting that if that young lad was set down in the Sahara he would draw a map of it. James was already envisaging his escape. He recognized that family was a net which one must flee, but he also knew that those stranded and imprisoned creatures, the passive mother, the furious father, the cowed and baffled brothers and sisters, were the potent material for his future works. For him as for Sophocles, great stories began in the family cauldron. He had seen a lot and a lot was required of him. As his young brother George was dying in the house of peritonitis and crying, "I am too young to die," James sat at the piano and played a tune which he had composed for a Yeats poem; a lyric which he regarded as the most beautiful he had ever read: "Who will go drive with Fergus now / And pierce the deep wood's woven shade . . . ?"

He doubled as father and son to the grieving family. But

that night when everyone had gone to sleep he came back downstairs to look at the little corpse, and noted that the blue of his eyes was still visible under the lids that had been closed too late. This eerie tenderness with which his stories, *Dubliners*, would be infused was something he kept to himself. With everyone in the family he was distant. He read voraciously, borrowing books from Capel Street library and of course incurring the wrath of the librarian when he took out questionable material. Sometimes he sent his brother Stanislaus to get the book or to pawn something for him. He had conquered the household and was fearless of any strictures either from them or his teachers. The priests at Belvedere thought he might secure a job as a clerk in Guinness's brewery, his father thought he was cut out for the law. On a whim, he decided on medicine but really only dabbled in it and was at the same time considering traveling around England, a minstrel with a lute. He seldom went to lectures, prepared nothing at home, absented himself from examinations and walked the streets thinking up his epiphanies, the syllables worked and reworked to resemble "many hued prisms."

For all its squalor, he determined to observe the life around him, to write about it and fling it abroad "amid planetary music." He managed always to seem insouciant and if he had a sign on his person it would be "Beware of the miserare." He would outgrow "the grave of his childhood," or so he thought. To live, to err, fall, to indulge the "lust of the McLochlanns" which ran in his veins was his motto. Prostitutes did not cost much—"all prick and no pence" as the bawd in *Ulysses* would say when Stephen Dedalus enters the den of iniquity. According to Stanislaus, one prostitute in the brothel where Joyce went was so fond of him that she offered him money to enter for a singing competition but he was "too fecking proud" to take it. He was proud. When it was pointed out to him that his name was up on a board at the university college because of his fees not being paid he affected blindness.

Discovering Ibsen ranks for Joyce as definitive as Saint Paul's conversion on the way to Damascus. Ibsen he placed above Shakespeare as a dramatist, Ibsen he revered because of his contempt for falsity and hypocrisy. A letter written to Ibsen's translator reveals Joyce the intending warrior identifying with Ibsen's battles, those as he said "fought and won behind your forehead." Ibsen had set an example to him to walk in the light of his inner heroism. "But we always keep the dearest things to ourselves," he wrote, a telling confidence sent to a famous man who was unable to read English and a poignant admission of how emotionally bereft Joyce really was. The equivocation, the sarcasm, the hauteur was merely a mask. At the end of the letter he wrote, "Your work on earth draws to a close and you are near the silence. It is growing dark for you." He was nineteen at the time. Young men do not usually know such things unless there is already on them a premonition of their own darkness. The rows, the deaths, the hunger, a constant scraping for money had been his bitter schooling and led to disdain for family and for country. Coming away from a play by Sudermann in which a family were pitilessly dissected, he told his parents that they need not have gone, the genius that they had seen on stage was breaking out in the home and against the home. He warned that it would happen in their own life.

For amusement, he wrote reviews of plays either in the manner of Carlyle, Macaulay or Cardinal Newman and then next day compared his with the review in the paper written by some ignoramus. This lack of intellectual vigor he classed as the "venereal condition of the Irish." He made no secret of his repulsion for the intellectual torpor around him and the craven adherence to mother church. Like the wild geese he wanted to go elsewhere. He wanted to be continentalized. He had a dream of Paris—that "lantern in the wood of the world for lovers." He remembered his dreams and transcribed some of them into a copybook. They have all the marks of a prodigal and disturbed imagination—a fairy-tale landscape full of mist and snow threatened by the presence of a beast, an archetype which he has to conquer. One beast muttered words he did not yet understand which of course prefigured his own assault on language, his dizzying escalations, words strung together to take on another light, another luster; multiple meanings, the wayward litanies of one who chose to believe that Jesus was more son of God than of Mary.

He broke with the Catholic Church while he was still in his teens but in another sense he never left it, he couldn't, the indoctrination from mother and priests had been too intense. On both mothers he would wage open and unrepentant war, calling the Catholic Church "the scullerymaid of christendom." The sermons of the priests filled him with terror and then repugnance. Jackpriests he called them, bullying, excoriating in their snorted Latin, tonsured and oiled, their bodies burly and "fat with the fat of kidneys of wheat." They had spoken of the damned falling into hell like hailstones and in one memorable outburst a priest had told them that if all the ills of the world, all the wars of the world and all the evils of the world could be avoided by the committing of one venial sin, it was still better that that venial sin be not committed. It was preposterous.

In *A Portrait of the Artist* Stephen Dedalus would say, "I

tried to love God" but implicit in this defection is his revulsion for God's ministers. Poets were the keepers of spirituality and priests the destroyers and usurpers. The bodies of the damned crying out for mercy, their tongues balls of fire, were as real to him as the flames of hell so vividly described. Escape it he did but leaving the Church is not the same as leaving God. Religious motifs would permeate his work, the sermon in *Portrait of the Artist* would send shivers through the sensibilities of future readers and parodies of prayer and ejaculation would be strewn in his work both in defiance of, and in homage to, his raving mentors. He would carry his work "like a chalice" and all his life he would insist that what he did "was a kind of sacrament." Father, Son and Holy Ghost along with Jakes McCarthy informed every graven word. On a more secular note he liked blackberry jam because Christ's crown of thorns came from that wood and he wore purple cravats during Lent.

Rebellion

OF ALL THE GREAT Irish writers, Joyce's relationship with his country remains the most incensed and yet the most meditative. Beckett, a much more cloistered man, was unequivocal; he made France his home and eventually wrote in French and though his elegiac works carry the breath of his native land, he did not expect Foxrock, his birthplace, to be etched in the consciousness of the world. Joyce did. He determined to reinvent the city where he had been marginalized, laughed at and barred from literary circles. He would be the poet of his race. In one of his early verses he likened himself to a stag, antlers charging upon the land.

J. M. Synge regretted every night he had lived out of Ireland and Yeats believed that the spirit of the ancients was his birthright and the inner source of his poetry whereas Joyce's birthright was a plaster virgin in Fairview, perched fowl-wise on a pole, the smell of rotting vegetables and a confraternity of rotting souls. To call this man angry is too temperate a word, he was volcanic. No one who has not lived in such straitened and hideous circumstances can understand the battering of that upbringing. All the more because they had come down in the world, a tumble from semi-gentility, servants, a nicely laid table, cut glasses, a piano, the accoutrements of middle-class life, relegated to the near slums in Mountjoy Square, the gaunt spectral mansions in which children sat like mice in the gaping doorways. It would be a downfall as far-reaching as Humphrey Chimpden Earwicker's disgrace in Phoenix Park once his sexual misdeed is put about.

The young James would walk across the sloblands of Fairview thinking and reciting "the silver-veined prose" of Cardinal Newman in an endeavor to banish from his mind the sparring household, the enamel basin in which he had washed himself and the kitchen clock which was one hour and twenty-five minutes fast. His journey led him along the water-logged lanes, past rubbish, offal, dripping trees, corner shops, a stone-cutting works that recalled the spirit of his hero Ibsen, and the docks in which the black arms of the tall ships told of distant nations, places he longed to escape to. He would never relinquish the anger that he felt then, revolt at the sight of the gray block of Trinity College "set heavily in the city's ignorance," or the statue of Thomas Moore, the national poet, covered in vermin. Even the guileless flower girl entreating him to buy flowers exasperated him and reinforced his fury over his own poverty. No Proustian madeleine would summon up this rigorous landscape. For him, as Auden would say of Yeats, "Mad Ireland hurt you into poetry."

The priests warned his mother of his waning faith, calling him an infidel because he refused confession or communion, and she knew without knowing that he had fallen into mortal sin. Her influence over him was gone. Packing his secondhand clothes as he prepared to set out for Paris she told him of her prayer, that away from home he might learn what the heart is and what it feels. Piety and sentiment he spat on. It unnerved and disgusted him. Just as his country did. He left it, so he said, for fear he might succumb to the national disease which

was provincialness, wind-and-piss philosophizing, crooked-
ness, vacuity and a verbal spouting that reserved sentiment for
God and for the dead. But though he had taken himself emotionally away from his mother he was haunted by her memory
and bore her a grudge that persisted to her deathbed and ever
after.

Her letters to him in Paris are a cry for reconciliation and her
own strangled longing for recognition. She was not, she wished
him to know, as stupid as he thought her to be and her ignorance was not for want of a longing desire to better herself.
Here was a woman over forty, ten children living, five dead, a
husband who invariably drank his pay packet, writing to her
gifted son of his ambitions and the prospects which lay ahead
for him. Her solicitude is heartbreaking: he is not to touch the
drinking water unless it is filtered or boiled. She assures him
that another money order will be sent the moment she can get
some. That she had the time let alone the stamina, when she
was already, though unknownst to herself, a dying woman,
makes the letters all the more poignant.

His letters veer from arrogance to self-pity. He is cold, unsettled and cannot afford an oil stove. He has not eaten for
forty-eight hours. Once he starts his medical studies he will
need further money for a white coat and dissecting utensils. He
asks for books to be sent, a copy of a British songbook along
with Wagner's operas, and reminds her to tell Stanislaus to retrieve some books from a pawnshop. With a mindless insou-
ciance he informs her that his friend (and enemy) Oliver St.
John Gogarty wrote to say that another friend had remarked
that there was "something sublime in Joyce's standing alone."
She wires money when she can wheedle it from her husband

though it means depriving the other children of food or clothes. She has had to sell a carpet to send the next installment and he hopes blithely that it is not the new carpet. Her eyes are so bad she can hardly see. Her young daughter May also has eye trouble and both pay visits to the eye hospital. He suggests that they get proper prescription glasses, failing to suggest where the money might come from. She is scolded for having once wired the money on a Saturday as it could not be cashed on Sunday. Moreover, the buttons in his good trousers have fallen off. She says he must not worry as she will have a new suit made for him. He would like it to be blue and asks if she could also enclose a blue felt hat. Blue was a color which had for him, with his host of superstitions, a talismanic significance. It was the color of his eyes and the color which would grace the cover of the first edition of *Ulysses*, that "obscene" book which would have killed her had she not already died. To his family of brothers and sisters his work was nothing short of betrayal. When he wrote of the snot-green sea, the snot was as much part of his daily imagery as the sea and so was the blood of the crushed dead lice under a mother's fingernails, but families do not see it like that, they can't. The writer exposes and reinforces their shame in themselves and they cannot forgive it.

That his mother loved him as she would a suitor is evident in every line of hers and he obliges by assuming a cavalier role. The pudding she proposes to send must be in a strong box and securely packed so as not to be opened by the customs. From time to time he allows for a word of thanks, gaily mentioning a supper followed by a cigar, then a box of confetti which he threw in the streets since it was carnival time. Drink is not alluded to or the "Scorta"—the prostitutes whom he went with and wrote lewd anatomical descriptions of, in dog Latin, to his roistering medical cronies. These were dispatched on post-cards which bore a photograph of himself, Rimbaud-like, in a long coat, the bohemian rake savoring the decadence of Paris. One friend, J. F. Byrne, was so shocked by these scatological bulletins that he temporarily broke off with Joyce. His punishment came later when he appeared thinly disguised as a priggish would-be prelate in *A Portrait of the Artist as a Young Man*.

Meanwhile Mrs. Joyce was assured that her studious son was teaching pupils, attending vespers at Notre Dame or St.-Germain, was reading Aristotle's *Metaphysics*, intending to have his first comedy published in five years and his "Aesthetic" five years after that. Not once did she question his gall or his arrogance. Instead she tries to skim over the adversities at home and asks that he write to his father in future because John is hurt by being left out of things. Her letters are amazing testaments to her love for him and they are as well the first glimpse of the galloping unpunctuated style which would become Molly Bloom's distinctive trademark. Speaking of her son Charlie, she says, "dont allude to this letter from me which is purely for his good and private he believes implicitly in you and all you say to him." It is often supposed that Nora Barnacle, Joyce's future sweetheart and wife, was the inspiration for Molly Bloom and while much of Molly's libido originates from Nora, the stream of prose devoid of commas and with the occasional arbitrary full stop is the creation of May Joyce. When not speaking of him or the family she showed a tartness in her nature. She urged him to make friends and if possible influential friends. She suggested that he cultivate Maud Gonne, who had just married John McBride, adding that marriage and lovemaking would naturally keep Madame McBride from looking after her more serious business. By that she meant Maud Gonne's politics. Maud Gonne was a fervent Irish nationalist, a Sinn Féiner whom Joyce referred to as the "Intensities" and the mythic Kathleen ni Houlihan, as "gap-toothed." Mother and son shared the same qualified view of the human race.

Monstrously indifferent to her reality, he seems only to have grasped it when in some letter she alludes faintly to her ailing health. He writes back and says to let him know what is wrong. Not long after came the never-failing heartrending cryptic Irish telegram—"Mother dying, come home." It was Good Friday night and he had to borrow the boat fare from one of his pupils. On that boat journey, he mused not on the dying woman but on the Paris boulevards, the prostitutes with their perfumed bodies and warm humid smells, then the gray engines, the mist over the French cliffs and the movements of the sea creating a corresponding music inside his brain. The artist had taken precedence over the son.

Her slow death from cancer is a tableau of cruelty and melodrama, and yet another definitive moment in the life of this haunted young man. Her brown grave clothes lay on the chair beside her and she picked at imaginary buttercups on the quilt and spoke in a wandering voice to a doctor who was not there. Baby, the youngest child, who was nine at the time, begged to be let into the room and John Joyce, at the end of his wits, told the woman to die and be done with it. May's brother pleaded with James and Stanislaus to kneel by the dying woman and promise to go to confession and communion as part of their Easter duty but neither of them would submit. In *A Portrait of the Artist* it resurfaces as Cranly upbraids the callous Stephen for not acceding to his mother's dying wishes and Stephen retaliates with "I will not serve." Pressed on matters of faith, he says that he neither believes nor disbelieves in the Eucharist.

Among his mother's girlish mementos were the early love letters John had written to her. Joyce took them into the garden where he could read them at his leisure to see if they were of any use for his future writings. Deciding they were not, he and Stanislaus burned them. It was a hasty thing to do and especially for the would-be writer who noted and hoarded every iota and even boasted that he put into his books the great talkers and the things they forgot. It has been suggested that they revealed a dark secret. May had come back from her honeymoon pregnant and though it was never openly referred to, there was that insinuation.

Death however neither burns nor kills the memory mother and in his fiction she was to come back to torment him again and again, her cerements shaken off, her glazing eyes staring at him from beyond death to shake and bend his soul. On him alone. It was as if he were an only child, which in a sense he felt he was, while also depicting himself as a foster son. That he was afraid of her is undoubted, and that he did everything to repress that fear is equally certain, but her effect on him was far-reaching. A prostitute's lingual kiss, the Host on the tongue and his mother's tenderness had been the three symbols battling for his soul. If she had not died then, he would for his art have had to kill her. Writers and their mothers—the uncharted deep.

Orphans

_____

FOR THE LARGE and motherless family it was a case of flits by moonlight as they moved house again and again to avoid landlord and bailiff, their possessions getting scantier and scantier so that it was no longer a horse-drawn dray but a hand-cart for the cups and saucers, a few articles of clothing and the family portraits of John Joyce's ancestors. In a short time they would have to move again before the new landlord—"his lordship"—caught up with them and often to buoy their spirits in these nighttime escapades the father would lead them into song:

> Shall carry my heart to thee
> Shall carry my heart to thee
> And the breath of the balmy night
> Shall carry my heart to thee.

They lived on credit loans and anything they could pawn. The family diet was tea, fried bread and dripping, the humors between the men caustic, their arguments fired by hangover, their repartee quick, unaffectionate and bitter. There were six sisters, the youngest, Baby, still howling to be reunited with her mother. Three of the men drank, John, James and Charlie, a younger brother. Stanislaus along with Poppy the eldest girl strove to keep the household together. At fifteen she had to beg from her father and pray that on the day he got his pension money he would bring some of it home. James came and went. He stayed with friends or with cousins and was often evicted because of his vagabond ways. He had a definitive sojourn with Gogarty in a Martello tower, formerly a bastion built by the British against Napoleonic invasion and named after Cape Mortella on Corsica. The short story was wild and bibulous, coopers of porter brought up the rope ladder which served as a stairs and caustic argument. Gogarty liked to get Joyce drunk in the hope that it would thwart his genius. It ended with Samuel Trench firing a revolver above Joyce's makeshift cot and so the "wandering Aengus" got up and left in the rain. Gogarty would appear as "Stately, plump Buck Mulligan" in the opening line of *Ulysses*, holding his shaving bowl aloft and intoning *Introibo ad altare Dei."* Jealous from the outset, Gogarty always saw himself as an "accessory" and took a loathsome revenge after Joyce's death.

Joyce was a master borrower and tried to raise a fund for himself by being reimbursed for his witticisms by his fellow medical students. When a friend or an acquaintance came to have a loan returned James countered with a bit of logic: "molecules change, other I borrowed money, I other I now." Once when he approached John Yeats, the father of the poet, for a "touch" of two shillings, Mr. Yeats said vehemently that he did not lend money to drunkards. Far from being embarrassed, he derided Yeats as being given to superfluous argument. He made many mistakes but said that a man of genius makes no mistakes and that all his actions however feckless, however cruel, are portals of discovery. He had to quit the medical school because of lack of funds but as well there was perhaps a lack of conviction. At different points in his life he thought of being a professional singer and actor and a traveling minstrel. He wrote to Arnold Dolmetsch, who had made a Psaltery for Yeats, to make him a lute so that he could go from Falmouth to Margate singing old English songs. Dolmetsch sent a frosty reply. His schemes were absurd. For him and the large family of brothers and sisters the reality was scutter and noserags and bread-and-dripping. He wore secondhand breeches which of course belonged to some poxy bowsy, which in turn would infect him. Drink, the Irish opium, was his solace. Only the sacred pint could unbind his tongue and naturally an excess of sacred pints had him prostrated in his "mulberrycoloured, multicoloured, multitudinous vomit."

John Joyce's moods vacillated between pathos and anger. He wept for his wife as he had not wept for her when she lived and he tyrannized the weaker members of his family. Stanislaus in his diary said that his most constant memory of his father was of John sitting at the kitchen table, not exactly drunk, grinding his teeth and muttering "Better finish it now." Finish what? His own life or theirs? In fact he lived into his eighties and his last words were to his favorite son: "Tell Jim he was born at six in the morning." A Dublin astrologer, hearing of this, drew up James's chart and predicted that a life of high risk was indicated. As an epitaph it could not be bettered. While all the other children lived in fear of him, James mocked his father. He saw him as "Mr Himmyshimmy, a blighty, a reeky, a lighty, scrapy, a babbly, a ninny, dirty seventh among thieves and always bottom sawyer." A swain, John had insisted on keeping photographs of former sweethearts on display and when Dante, a housekeeper, burnt them, May Joyce was lambasted. John Joyce also boasted to have cured himself of syphilis.

A Cork man, the only child of an only child, John in his heyday was a cock of the walk wherever he went. His singing voice, as he liked to remind his boozing friends, had been compared to the Italian tenor Campanini, the toast of Covent Garden and New York. In drink he waxed sentimental, glorifying the old days, the great days when as a youngster he followed the hounds in County Cork or excelled at rowing in the regattas in Dublin Bay. Drink was his liberator. Describing a drinking bout after the results of an election in which a Home Rule candidate was returned, he boasted how he and his friends so impatient for drink could not wait for the corks to be drawn but broke the necks of the bottles of champagne on the marble-topped counters. His hero was Charles Stewart Parnell, an austere and iconoclastic Anglo-Irish man revered in Ireland as the "Risen Christ" and the "Uncrowned King," a Moses leading the Irish people to the promised land of Home Rule. His speeches in the House of Commons struck fear into both Tories and Liberals. Then overnight his downfall when it was revealed that he had had a long-standing affair with Kitty O'Shea, wife of an Irish captain and already mother to two of Parnell's "bastards." Those who had served him and those who had worshiped him now turned on him, including his secretary and colleague in Westminster, Tim Healy. The young Joyce, appalled by such betrayal, wrote with his father's help an ode entitled "Et Tu, Healy." The priests denounced Parnell from the altar, the laity threw quicklime in his eyes, and his reputation was so destroyed that no member of his party stood a hope of reelection. When the elections did come the clergy insisted that the faithful were unable to read the names on the ballot sheet and had instructed them to do the voting for them. Parnell's life as a

politician was finished and within a year he was dead. His funeral of thirty thousand people was the largest ever seen in
Dublin; as John Joyce remarked bitterly, "A dead Irishman was
more popular than a living one."

By terrorizing his children, John alienated all of them, all
except James, who was a sinner like himself. Stanislaus hated
his father, hated his self-love, his vanity and his raving outbursts as he threatened to break their hearts, to break their
bloody hearts and their bloody arses with it. His family was his
empire. The brutality he meted out to them was probably not all
that different from other households in Dublin with a chronic
shortage of money and a litter of children. It was not that he was
without emotion, he simply did not know what to do with it.
Domination of them reaffirmed his powers as a man. He would
take the nearest thing, a poker, a plate, a cup, and fling it at
whatever child roused his rage. The girls were so afraid of him
that they would beg Stanislaus or James not to go out in the evening and leave them alone with a fitful father. It was left to
Stanislaus to stay behind because James by then had started
on his libertine ways, quaffing, roistering with his university
friends and frequenting the brothels in "Nighttown." John
swore that he would finish him with three kicks on the arse, oh
yes, three kicks but it was a vain boast. His father could not
break him because James had made himself invincible. The
language exchanged between them was the language of Dublin
tenements—pissabed, arse, whore bloody corner boy, bloody
nigger, bloody mulatto . . .

Warring sons and sacrificial daughters stranded in their
separate ways and having to school themselves against the
"therrble prongs" of life. But it was true for John too. He was a

broken man, his life devoid of hope. On the evening of their mother's funeral when James and friends repaired to a public house, Stanislaus confronted his father, blaming him not only for the mother's death, but for George's also, who was buried in Glasnevin with the mother and the siblings, not far from where Parnell lay, as aloof in death as he had been in life. As Stanislaus hurled these accusations at him John replied with a rejoinder, wretched as King Lear's. Stanislaus insisted that the deaths could have been avoided if the father, instead of squandering his money on drink, had gone and got a decent doctor. John tried to defend himself, listing the mortgages he had taken out on the properties owned in Cork to pay for all the family illnesses down the years, but Stanislaus was not to be silenced. John looked at him then, recognized the bitter intent and simply said, "You don't understand, boy." To have come down in the world was a bitter blow, deprived as he was of life's luxuries and robbed of the esteem of his former friends. The shame of being poor runs deep in the Irish psyche. The famine times were only fifty years earlier, times when families closed their doors rather than let the world see them die of starvation. Evictions had been as recent as fifteen or twenty years before, when whole families were thrown onto the roadside, their cabins razed by the battering ram. These terrible fates they saw not as the work of the invader but as a consequence of their own fecklessness.

When John lost his job as a rates collector because of misdemeanors and discrepancies in his paperwork, it struck at the entire family. May went in secret to the authorities to ask to have it restored and was turned away. He did receive a miserly pension but from then on it was moneylenders, furniture put up as collateral, mortgages on his three small properties in Cork and, most shaming of all, his name in *Stubbs' Gazette* and *Perry's Weekly* where he was blacklisted as a debtor. It would haunt him and it would mark his son indelibly for life. Profligate he may have been, but James worried about money to the end. Even if he had been wealthy he would have believed himself to be destitute. Two days before his death in 1941, as he was about to undergo an operation, he asked his son plaintively who would pay for it. His funeral expenses and a contribution to his father's funeral expenses before him were paid by an English benefactress, Harriet Shaw Weaver, one of the galaxy of serving "women in wait" whose cause in life was to further the genius of James Joyce.

In his youth James was deaf to the cries of his family, knowing that if he had listened he would have been swallowed up by them. He determined to live vicariously, or as Stanislaus ruefully put it, he made living his end in life. Nevertheless the secret life of his mind was already in full and prodigious spate. He was notorious in the bars, an arrogant young man in frayed clothes, white rubber shoes and a yachting cap, eager to parry, to dissimulate, to discuss Euclid or Aquinas or Nelly the Whore and to warn adversaries that he would lampoon them in his satirical verses. So sure was he of his gifts that he had written to Lady Augusta Gregory, who was at the helm of the Irish literary revival, assuring her that he meant one day to be "somebody." The story goes that he called on W. B. Yeats at a hotel in Rutland Square and sympathized with Yeats, who was thrity-seven on that day, as being too old to learn from him. His talents, he said, would burn "with a hard and a gem-like ecstasy." That he was insufferable is probably true, but that he had the trepid intensity of a poet was also true, he who walked in the violet night "beneath a reign of uncouth stars." He generated envy. Stanislaus envied him the purity of his intention. In his diary he observed everything James did, everything James said, conceding that he might have genius, then retracting it, believing James to be too reckless, too unsettled. Stanislaus, nicknamed "Brother Stan" on account of his ponderousness, seemed to take on all the woes and humiliations of the family. He admitted that James used him as a butcher uses a whetstone to sharpen his knife. How terrible it was to have a cleverer elder brother and, moreover, one who held him in as much regard as he might an umbrella.

Samuel Beckett in his essay on Jack Yeats wrote that the artist who stakes his life has no brother and comes from nowhere. It may be true for the artist but it is not true for the brother. All his life Stanislaus persisted in the belief that he deserved a share in James's renown. As they fell asleep in the same bed at night and spoke that flotsam of speech which comes just before sleep—"the a-a-a-ahs . . . what's his name . . . can't think"—Joyce hit on an innovative daring, the uninterrupted unrolling of thought which was to be the radical innovativeness of *Ulysses*. While Stanislaus knew that Jim was wayward, he was as well a very "Yggdrasil," the great ash tree symbolic of the universe in Norse mythology. Everything about Jim obsessed him. The very opening words of his diary are: "Jim's character is unsettled; it is developing. New influences are coming over him daily, he is beginning new practices. He has come home drunk three or four times within the last month (On one occasion he came home sick and dirty-looking on Sunday morning, having been out all night) . . ." To say that Stanislaus was obsessed with James is an understatement, he wanted to be him. It has happened in more than one writing family. That spark of genius given to one and not to all.

Revels

AT THAT TIME in Dublin prostitution was carried on as publicly as in Algiers. The clientele were sailors, British Tommy army officers, and privates who went in closed cabs at night. Last but not least were the medical students, the jolly old medicals, and Joyce the lapsed medical student among them. So limp with leching, they betook themselves to the pelvic basin of the icky licky micky red-light district in the Ringsend Road where hung out Fresh Nelly, Rosalie and the coalquay whore.

> I gave it to Nelly
> To stick in her belly
> The leg of the duck
> The leg of the duck.

No doubt the brothels did not have the mad carnival fascination that Joyce later endowed them with, but they were where he found his much-desired abasement. The one singled out in *Ulysses* was run by Mrs. Bella Cohen whose main ambition in life was to send her son to Oxford. Stephen Dedalus engages in a Saturnalian debauch, conjoins with this woman or that, one with gold stibbled teeth, another with leg-of-mutton sleeves, still another with a little brown scapular of the Lamb of God to keep her from sin. "Goaded, buttocksmothered" he derives little pleasure from his couplings, only consternation. The women are too frightening, too menacing; even those with little soft palms are capable of vivisecting a man or putting stars and stripes on his breeches. It is a carnal hell. Stephen is made to confront his dead mother in leper gray, reminding him that she thinks of him in death and causing him to shout out "Nothung!" and smash a lamp with his ashplant.

Venturing into the gloomy secret night, watching the prostitutes setting out for their trade, pinning up their hair and giving him the come-hither, was a prologue to the swelling act. Stanislaus tells us in his diary that the one called Nelly who wanted to loan Joyce money to enter the singing competition would accompany him on the chamber pot as he practiced his scales and sang his favorite songs. A long way that from the concert hall or Yeats' Kiltartan and the heroic cycles of the great Fianna race. Nevertheless Joyce had a certainty about what he would do and his strength coupled with his dissipation is staggering. He genuinely believed that he should be supported at the expense of the State because he was so capable of enjoying life. "O strive not to be excellent in woe" was a line from Dowden's poem which he addressed to himself and later to Nora Barnacle, the woman he would fall in love with. She was to separate him from his family or so they liked to believe, loath to admit that he would have gone anyhow. "Miss Barnacle has a very pretty manner, but the expression of her face seems to me a little common," Stanislaus wrote tartly in his diary. Joyce kept it a secret until he knew what he really felt about her.

All the time he was writing fragments of his autobiographical novel *Stephen Hero*, the character of Dedalus transmuting into Proteus, he who could change his shape at will. On his walks along Sandymount strand Joyce accumulated the images for his work, sea spawn and sea wrack, the nearing tide, the rusted boat skeletons; cockle pickers sousing their bags; his reveries interrupted with classical interjection, musings, escalations, remorse at his mothers's death, salivation at the thought of the libertine gypsies and occasional spasms of fear of the shawled whores in the archways, a "shefiend's whiteness" under their "rancid rags." He ruminated as well on the potbellied Thomas Aquinas, Aristotle bald and thin-legged inheriting a fortune from his pupil Alexander the Great, and the fading prophecies of Joachim Abbas. Joyce's learning was prodigious. It has been said by his great biographer, Richard Ellmann, that he had read everything by the time he was twenty. Ineluctable modality of all things visible was his visionary aim. Who can blame him if in that spate of high-hearted youth and virtuosity he likened himself to Parnell, Hamlet, Dante, Byron, Lucifer and Jesus Christ? Gravity and despair were for much later on. The Golden Fleece was his. He had snatched it unbeknownst to his literary friends and he himself would be the dragon to guard it against all predators.

He was a man who believed in the portents—names, numbers, mattered to him and he was able to read hidden augury in a shooting star or the passage of a flight of seabirds. The young girl he was about to meet bore the same name as the wild goose—Nora Barnacle, a Galway girl who had run away from her family after a brutal beating by a jealous uncle because of her seeing a local Protestant boy. In the encyclopedia, barnacles were described as "warm-blooded, vertebrated animals with four-chambered hearts and limbs that metamorphosed into wings." Feathers as phantasmagoric as those surrounding Calypso's cave. A Galway girl with an affiliation to Homer's epic. Joyce longed to copulate with the soul. What we long for, it seems we sometimes get.

Nora

STANISLAUS SAID that if James longed to copulate with a soul he ought to get himself born anywhere other than Ireland. But Stanislaus was mistaken. His brother fell "unto tiptition—O Charis! O Charissima! A more intriguant bambolina could one not colour up out of Boccuccia's Enameron. . . . The myth inmid the air. Mother of moth." Was she jaunty, auburn-haired Nora Barnacle, sauntering into his life, on the tenth of June as he walked down Nassau Street in torn canvas shoes, wielding an ashplant? They stopped to talk. She thought his blue eyes were those of a Scandinavian and he liked that, believing he had Danish blood in his veins. He was twenty-two and she was twenty. They made a date to meet four days later at No. 1 Merrion Square, outside the house where Sir William Wilde lived. Standing on that corner Joyce had the dubious advantage of being able to see in four different directions but no Nora came up the street or jumped off a tram. He wrote to her that night and said that he had looked for a long time at a reddish-brown crop of hair and regretfully had to concede that it was not hers. Might they have another appointment? His tone was light but his intention determined.

To have an inkling of anyone else's ascension-descension into love is almost impossible but in the case of James Joyce it is confounding. Here there was no truck with pots and pans, no engagement ring, no pandering to the family members, no normality. Though his amorous adventures had been solely with women "on the turf," he had also sustained the dream of women as idealized creatures on pedestals, put there for his litanies alone. Women were like rivers that flowed in their own ineluctable way. "Teaseforhim. Toesforhim. Tossforhim." Exultance. Idiosyncrasy. Fate. He asked himself what Caesar might have lived to do had he believed the soothsayer and his wife, Calpurnia, and not gone out on the Ides of March. It was ordained. He was tired of "scortatory love" and whores were bad conductors of emotion. So it was not with a casual comrade in lust that the entrails of his soul would be laid bare but with a fairly illiterate Galway girl who was plucky enough to leave her own family and find employment as a chambermaid in Finn's Hotel in Dublin.

In her he was to seek and find earth mother, dark, formless, made beautiful by moonlight. He was a Dubliner, she was from Galway; she was to bring in her jingles, her stories, her piseogs the echoes of her ancestry, the other half of Ireland—soil, gloom, moon gray nettles, the warring clans and the mutinous Shannon waters. Yeats had said that when he fell in love with Maud Gonne it was when all the troubling of his life began. For Joyce it was the opposite, this young girl was a summons to his blood. They met a few nights later on June 16, an encounter so important to Joyce and so consequential that he was to set *Ulysses* on that very same day and the world would come to call it Bloomsday after its hero Leopold Bloom.

His letters written to her in the morning would, miraculously, be delivered before lunch and he would have a reply before nightfall. She would run from her duties to the bedroom, or the WC, and learn that she was to leave her stays at home because they were like a dragoon's, that she was to come without skirts in order to receive his papal benediction, a power of indulgence which had been vested in him by Pope Pius X. She must know that it was from such muddy pools that angels called forth a spirit of beauty. He was drinking her mountain dew. He could not say that he loved her, he would not say it. She pressed. He would not say it. He could say that he was very fond of her, that he desired to possess her wholly, that he admired and honored her and that he sought to secure her happiness. Love it may not be, but need it was. She became the breast between him and God and death—"How I hate God and death! How I like Nora!"

He was, without knowing it, a committed man. He told her that he thought life was waiting for him if he chose to enter it but that it could not give him the intoxication that it once had given him. No human being ever stood so close to him as she stood. He honored her very much but he wanted more than her caresses. In his next letter he would contradict that. She was to be no casual comrade in lust. She must know that he had left the Catholic Church, hating it most fervently, that it had been impossible for him to remain part of it because of the impulses of his nature. Moreover, he would make open and unrepentant war on it. He railed against the friends who he believed had betrayed him and said scornfully that his brothers and sisters meant nothing to him. With each passing day he became more attached to her, wanting to know about Galway and its outskirts—woods, fields, cows, cowslips, herself and her companions undressing in the sunny hills and seeing their bodies as wild roses.

He tried to be her, to know her as in her convent days when the Sisters of Mercy prepared her for First Holy Communion, her scallywagging days when she made a date with an older man and then later with a girlfriend hid in a church and devoured the chocolates the man had given her. For her transgression she got a thrashing from her uncle. Joyce had to be told each and every thing, to strip her of all mask and all clothing, to pass through her, to know the secret of her. She did not shrink from this. She was glad to describe her little girlhood props, her garters, her bracelets and a brooch that looked like the lily-of-the-valley flower. He reveled in hearing the mischievous things that she did—putting a snood over her auburn hair, donning man's clothes and standing on a dungheap, chewing raw cabbage and hoping to hear the sound of the name of her future husband. On their very first night she had opened his trousers and her fondling had, as he put it, "made me a man." Yet when asking for greater favors on subsequent nights he saw that he had insulted her and felt "a terrible pre-aged melancholy in her eyes." She was his precious darling, his pouting Nora, his little brown head as well as being mother earth made beautiful by moonlight and only dimly conscious of her myriad fluid-like instincts. He loved her soft voice. In her company he put aside his jeering contemptuous nature. She was invited to the concert hall to hear him sing and to his mortification he had to dig out the notes for himself on the piano because the pianist had failed to show up. One of the songs he chose was "Down by the Sally Gardens" in which a confident young woman bids her young man to take love easy. Without knowing it, he was falling into that "untoward phenomenon" called love.

For entertainment they walked. They could not afford to do anything else. Yet he was not blind to what he saw—the watchtowers, the murmuring waters, the fishful stream and the empathy of the mighty dead. He was not to assign it to paper until long after but he saw and noted it all. He saw the space of the sky, the ever-changing evening violet, the dark dripping gardens with their ash pits, the soggy flower beds, the stables where a coachman combed the horses and of course the sea, the seaweed, the warm sand, the wavelets, the sharp shingle, the water mirroring the high drifting clouds. Next day she wrote to say that in his company she always felt herself to *be*, her spirit took leave of her body in sleep, and the loneliness which she felt in his absence faded away in his presence. He recognized at once that these high-flown sentiments were not the words of a country girl who invoked charms and made beds and emptied chamber pots for a living. He had guessed rightly. She had copied the letter from a book of etiquette at the time. He loved her even more—"God becomes man becomes fish becomes barnacle goose becomes featherbed mountain." Nora personified "the most beautiful and simple soul in the world." Her kisses were like the singing of canaries. He was her brother in luxuriousness, her Christian brother and agonizing Jew. As he saw more of her he felt obliged to tell her how much he hated and disavowed mother church and how he had caroused with the ladies of Nighttown. She did not want to know. She must. She would have to know how august he was and how flawed. She would have to know that he entered the social order of Ireland as a deliberate vagabond. There was Stephen the acolyte and Bloom the lecher and they alternated. One day it was her knickers and the next day it was his soul on the brink of hers and by morning it was himself making covert halfhearted plans to run away with an actors' company. But he was already bound to her. The proverb that Lermontov quotes in *A Turkish Tale* was true for Joyce also—"Whereupon is written upon a man's forehead at birth he is not fated to forgo." Maybe it was those dog's eyes of hers. Like Anne Hathaway, she hath a way. By cock she was to blame. She had put come hither on him. He would sleep with her glove beside him and had to remark that it behaved itself very properly, like its owner. He would buy her a gift of gloves but where to get the money? He hoped to be paid for a short story which had been accepted by the *Irish Homestead*, to which he gave the alternative title "Pigs' Paper." He was scrounging in the name of the crucified Christ and getting volleys of refusal. No rhymed with woe.

He knew that by becoming attached to such an unschooled country girl he would offend his own family and have to battle with every religious and social force in Ireland. She had already promised to stand beside him in his hazardous life and this filled him with pride and joy. His plan to leave Ireland and to leave with her was being hatched. He had answered an advertisement for a teaching post in a Berlitz school and was waiting intrepidly for the reply. Paris was where he hoped he would return and he amused himself at the thought of the stir it would cause in Dublin when people heard that he and Nora were living in sin in the Latin Quarter.

It was then his "touching" began in earnest. He sought help from the literary circles which he had harangued against. He asked Yeats if a fund could be raised for him at the Abbey Theatre and was refused. Next it was to Lady Gregory for five pounds to help him in his teaching abroad. She too declined, wanting evidence of a concrete plan, and nettled by her rejection he wrote back: "Now I will make my own legend and stick to it." She relented and sent the money. From others he asked for a few shillings, trousers, an old pair of shoes. A friend was told to get from his father's shop one toothbrush, tooth powder, a nailbrush, a pair of boots, a coat and a vest. He must have relied on Nora Barnacle to have her own toothbrush and tooth powder. She was expecting a little legacy from a grandmother in Galway, but it did not materialize. When they headed separately for the mail boat in the North Wall in Dublin, their elopement was shrouded in secrecy. Nora had to slip onto the boat unseen. On the quayside, the Joyce family had assembled for the inevitable parting glass. His brothers and sisters did know that James had a companion but John Joyce, ignorant of that treachery, presented his son with seven pounds and predicted for him a great future.

There were a few plaudits. Gogarty, with feigned sincerity, said he would "miss the touch of a vanished hand." The Provost of Trinity College, a Mr. Pentland Mahaffy, added his obituary. Comparing Joyce to the corner boys who spat in the Liffey he welcomed the departure but said that it was not before Joyce "had squirted his stinks" on his native city. For the twenty-two-year-old author Ireland would become the ferment for his imagination with those twin stalwarts, memory and exile, for good measure.

Exiles

In London Nora had her first taste of the uncertainty that would dog her whole life. Joyce had gone to call on Arthur Symons, a friend of Yeats, to discuss possible publication of his poems *Chamber Music*, while she sat on a park bench, wondering if her Norseman would return. Eventually he did. That night they set out for Paris with one suitcase, their money almost spent. It was more tenterhooks in Paris, Joyce going off to meet his old friends and to "touch" them for the fare to go on to Zurich. Although he was bound to her, he shrank from introducing her to his literary friends. By then his father had learned the horrible news as it was a topic in all the Dublin pubs and he raged not only at the defection but the harm that this relationship would do to his son's life. A brilliant future, as he said, was "blasted in one breath."

When they arrived in Zurich there was no vacancy in the Berlitz School, the Miss Gilford of Lincolnshire having deceived Joyce. They managed to stay one night in a guest house which bore the auspicious name of "Hope." It was there the "adventure" was consummated and James, still half-embroiled in the family matrix, told Stanislaus in a letter that she was no longer a virgin, she had been "touched." The pun can hardly have been lost on either of them. The bloodstains on the sheet, he was later in a moment of insane jealousy, to question. And later still Molly Bloom was to say drolly that any woman could simulate her virginity with a drop of red ink or blackberry juice. And so it was on to Trieste where there was no vacancy either, his skills as borrower sorely tried. He found two pupils to whom he gave English lessons. As usual there were some incidents. He managed to get himself arrested when he intervened in a fight between three drunken British sailors and was almost deported back to Ireland. In the midst of such precariousness he wrote the twelfth chapter of *Stephen Hero* and began a story called "Christmas Eve."

The head of the Berlitz School took pity on them and within a few days found a teaching post for Joyce in the naval town of Pola one hundred and fifty miles away. An official who met them at the boat said he did not know whether to contemplate murder or suicide, upon sighting a ragged couple dragging a torn suitcase with bits of clothing sticking out, "the bride" in a man's long overcoat and a straw hat pulled down over her head. Joyce was in his element—here was a milieu of several languages, a hotpotch of tongues, Italian, Serbian, German, all of which would be threaded into his future work. For Nora it was quite a different story. She felt lost, far from home and with no one to turn to, only her wayward liege. "James Joyce, Bachelor of Arts" proved to be an idiosyncratic teacher. His employers thought him gifted but also conceited and absurd, a man of contradictions, fragile and hysterical, refined and ascetic yet one who gravitated toward the mud. Soon they saw his great partiality for drink.

To Stanislaus he wrote almost daily, sent stories, extracts from his novel, conceding that only Stanislaus took him seriously. There were mounting complaints. Nora was homesick, lonely when he went out of the house and inept at picking up foreign languages. His belittling of her was his way of asking forgiveness. It was her or them, as he well knew. Were her family by any chance putting advertisements in the paper to ask of her whereabouts, did the girls who had worked with her in the hotel think her "snotty"? Stanislaus was to be told some of her most precious secrets, her early cavorts, a near seduction by a young curate with black curly hair, a thrashing from an uncle which developed into some kind of orgasmic fit. For one so quick to sense betrayal Joyce was master at it himself. Stanislaus was also importuned to raise money somehow and send it by return. There was a request as well for newspapers, Joyce's early epiphanies, a key to a trunk which he could not open, his BA certificate, his sheet music, Renan's *Life of Christ*, Nora's birth certificate and a copy of her grandmother's will which would be in the Record Office of the Law Courts in Dublin. The letters would be unpardonable if, behind them, one did not sense a man driven to distraction in this backwater, chronically short of money, teaching English, learning German, suffering a solitude of the intellect and sending sections of his novel home for Stanislaus to give an opinion on them. They were then to be passed on to Curran and Cosgrave, the very friends who envied him. Word would come that everyone was surprised about his elopement and George Russell, his former editor, wished him a touch of starvation.

What Joyce did not convey in his letters home was his prostrating himself before her, his appeal to her for God's sake that they not be unhappy, his very trembling if she gave him a cross look. Her powers over him were undoubted and her sexual powers were consummate. But as a companion in the world of burghers and schoolmasters she was a drawback. His colleagues wondered what he was doing with her, one of them even reducing her to a state of tears in a restaurant.

He earned two pounds a week by teaching English and Italian to officers of the Austrian Navy. He looked forward to the day when he could get a new suit and have his teeth fixed. They rose at nine and partook of chocolate, lunched in a *locanda* opposite and if they could afford it, had dinner at eight. Their staple was Turkish tobacco which they rolled themselves. When Nora became pregnant he started making halfhearted plans to leave her. He was telling Stanislaus that there was an anxiety at the back of his mind for which he would have to be prepared materially. And did Nora sense it? We will never know. She said to tell Stan, "She was axing for him." She put X's for kisses and vacillated between moroseness and high spirits.

She often sang when dressing, trying on different pairs of drawers in the wardrobe to tantalize him:

> "Old Tom Gregory
> Has a big menagerie . . ."

She licked the jam off its sealing-paper cover and regaled him with her droll country sayings. But there was a less sunny side to her. There was the helpless girl who hid in a dark room and cried. She was afraid to go out into the street without him, for fear of being insulted. She spoke thirty words of Triestine dialect, could not learn French and disliked Italian cooking, thinking it too sloppy. The Director of the Berlitz School said, upon meeting her, that she was not worthy of Joyce. But Joyce decided that only would-be thinkers or feminists would expect a woman to be a man's equal. For all his ribaldry about it, it was plain that there were problems. The heat made her breathless and powerless, the cold gave her chilblains. She often said that she longed to hear and see a kettle boiling on a hob. She moped. He feared that she was sapping his natural cheerfulness. So here we have this young girl, in a short brown dress, with cinders in her hair, living with a man whose body she could enrapture but whose mind she could not fathom. He saw that she was one of those plants that could not be safely transplanted. He feared for the moroseness of the child that she would bring forth and felt pity as he watched her fail to make the baby clothes that she was trying desperately to copy from a pattern. She was weakening his natural cheerfulness and hearing mistakenly that Ibsen had left his wife, the same thought occurred to him. They spent nights of horrible melancholy, one of which she salvaged for him by quoting a line of his poetry—"O Sweetheart, hear you/ Your lover's tale." She had misquoted it but her very utterance had miraculously revived his flagging belief in himself as a poet. Also their estrangements were a spur to their lusts. But he was restless. To Stanislaus he broached the idea of returning home, smarting under the degrading and unsatisfactory nature of his exile. He longed for a slice of boiled leg of mutton with turnips and carrots. He did not foresee a lengthy future with Nora and was not one of those who believed in living together in a state of "mutual tolerance." The fact that she was pregnant made everything more tentative. While deciding that he and Nora would possibly have to part, he was at the same time suggesting to Stanislaus that the three of them rent a nice thatched cottage in the Dublin suburbs. He added some beguiling flourishes—cottage roses and so forth. Above all, he wished to talk to someone. He had reached prostrating depths of boredom. Would Stanislaus come for even a week so that they could have a serious conversation?

They had reckoned that their first child was due in August but not unsurprisingly they had miscalculated the event. Joyce was about to go bathing when Nora was struck down with a pain that seemed remarkably like indigestion. Their landlady summoned the midwife. Six hours later, when he held his son and heir in his arms, he hummed operatic airs to it and predicted that it would have the singing voice of its father and its grandfather. This was a hope that he never forsook.

When the telegram "Son born Jim" reached Dublin in the early hours of the morning, the family wept and rejoiced. Stanislaus said that it had given him a "Christmas morning feeling" (it was July) and he was as well implored to go to a mutual friend called Curran because the jubilant father was in a slight fix. John Joyce also borrowed a pound to send to his son. Emotion and unwonted sentiment crossed back and forth between them. James confessed to a sense of staggering joy and said that the most important thing that could happen to a man was the birth of a child. Before Giorgio was born he had no fear of fortune, but now he had.

Christmas morning feelings don't last long. Soon Nora was taking in laundry—chemises, blouses, vests, items listed on the back of a short story which Joyce was writing at the time. It was called "A Little Cloud" and depicted strained relations between a man and wife as new love waned, the man imprisoned and driven to distraction by a wailing child. Years later, in *Finnegans Wake* two washerwomen would regale each other with the vices and wrongdoing of their customers. But Nora Barnacle had no washerwoman friend, no one to commune with, except her husband and then mostly in bed. Disenchanted by home life Joyce kissed one of his students, Annie Schleimer, even suggesting they might marry. When her father heard of it her classes were canceled at once.

To his students he was an anarchist—lively, eccentric, profane. He regaled them with what he called "vignettes": The owner of the Berlitz School was an insatiable sponge who soaked up the teachers' brains and crucified their flesh. A certain lady with small breasts had a conscience large as a sewer. To develop the self he suggested they take his example and suck up fourteen shots of absinthe on an empty stomach. All governments were pirates. Tax demands were little pieces of paper onto which he could scribble or his wife could jot down those nothings which mothers write for their children. A Dublin man, according to him, spent his time babbling in pubs and whorehouses and never tired of the same concoction of whiskey and promise of Home Rule. The Irish, doomed to express themselves in a language not their own, had stamped it with their genius and competed for glory with other civilized countries. It was called English literature. Samuel Beckett many years later improved on that, claiming that the Catholic Church and English domination had "buggered [Irish writers] into glory."

While Joyce might mock the drunken Dubliner to his students he was carrying on the tradition in faithful style, staying in the bars and "arsing" his way home at dawn. It was his way of practicing birth control and in one of these homilies he warned his wife, "No, no, Nora, my girl, I have little appetite for that game"—by which he meant sex and procreation. A few nights later it was a different story, he longed to sink into the womb of her being. He drank in tiny taverns called "Hole in the Wall" and often fell on the way home until some Samaritan came to rescue him. A fellow teacher, Alessandro Francini-

Bruni, describes himself as the Simon of Cyrene carrying the cross for a drunken Jesus. During these cavorts Joyce would be heard to sing, "Of the good stuff let's have more. Because I've lost the key to my door." It was useless to remonstrate with him.

Then and always he deferred to no one. Francini-Bruni describes his self-destruction as being cold and premeditated. Nora had to inure herself to the many and conflicting sides of his nature. She would threaten to leave and sometimes she did leave but she was bound to him, having burned her boats with her family and Galway and known to be living in sin. He would swear not to drink again and then break out the very next day. His mind was all fluxion, his head full of discordant ideas which crystallized into beautiful sequences of prose soaring from the mire to the summits of asceticism. As Francini-Bruni saw it, his soul was in chaos, a frail hysterical man, often seen to weep for his native land and for the thousands of tormented souls that had wept there over the centuries. He was scornful of politics, monarchies, republicans, kings, popes; he bowed to no one. Sometimes garrulous, other times sarcastic, his lips "tight together in a hard horizontal line" he ridiculed those around him.

He had kept imploring Stanislaus to join him so that they could have that serious conversation. Stanislaus demurred. James insisted. They would be a happy family together— James, Nora, little Giorgio and "dear sweet enchainted Stanislaus." James and Nora had moved to Trieste and he had found for his brother a teaching post in the Berlitz School where he himself taught. By pooling their resources they could get by comfortably enough and might even afford a piano. The enticements varied. Stanislaus would arrive just in time for the new wine and the roast chestnuts. As a last measure, he sent forty crowns for Stanislaus to buy himself some good clothes because of the cursed stupid snobs at the school.

For Stanislaus the sea voyage took thirty hours and the train journey across Europe two days. He had been sick on the sea and hungry on the long train journey. James met him at the station and said somewhat cursorily, "You are so changed I would have passed you in the street." When they got to the apartment, James told him that between him and Nora they possessed "one centesimo." It was not a warm welcome. Nora was suspicious of Stanislaus as she was of all the Joyce family. Stanislaus, almost twenty-one and of sober mien, was made to feel unwelcome in a small flat with a young child where daytime tetchiness contrasted with nighttime amorousness. He had been summoned not as brother but as underling. Joyce barely spoke to him. He was going through one of his more outraged periods. The institution of marriage or common-law marriage was not to his liking and to discuss it was quite useless. As soon as he got his salary he drank it. He drank Stanislaus's salary also and drank whoever's money he could borrow. Then, contrite over this and wanting to appease Nora, he would take whatever little was in the family kitty and buy her a gift. One evening, with the money intended for their supper, he ran out and procured a hand-painted silk scarf. She kept threatening to go back to Galway with Giorgio and as he looked over her shoulder while she penned her grievances, Joyce suggested icily that she should try using the capital letter for the word "I." He was not so intolerant of this lapse when he sat down to write Molly Bloom's galloping soliloquy.

So home atmosphere was trying: little to eat, creditors calling at unforeseen hours, Joyce managing to stall by striking up a tune on the piano and Stanislaus sent scurrying to the Berlitz

School to borrow from one professor or another. Comedy it may seem in retrospect but for each of them it was a trial.

In his diary Stanislaus tells us that he saved them from starvation many times. Yet he never left. Like Nora, he threatened to. She seems to have shown little sympathy for him, at least in those early years. Her view was that if Stanislaus could provide money it was fine but if he wanted to hoof off, "Ah, let him go." He moved for short periods but like all emotional mendicants he came back. Something bound Stanislaus to his brother and it can hardly be called love. James had become surrogate father and living persecutor. Writing home, Stanislaus tried to convey his anguish but not being a poet he simply said that he missed the sound of the foghorns in Dublin Bay.

Manifesto

"FOR THE LOVE OF the Lord Christ, change my curse-o'-God state of affairs." Change, change—it was wine, frankincense and myrrh to him. Stanislaus saw how James throve "on the excitement of events"; and Richard Ellmann was to describe Joyce's life as moving from "crisis to crisis, exacerbation to exacerbation." Trieste where he had lived for four years was drab, provincial, boiling summers that turned men such as himself into butter, the hateful "Bora" wind roaring away and gassing provincial windbags—in short, a reminder of Dublin. Moreover, having Stanislaus come to live with him and Nora was a severe handicap. Stanislaus had served perfectly as the one to write letters to, to discourse with on this and that, to evaluate fragments of work which James sent him, but Stanislaus under the same roof, groaning on about responsibility and thumping his famous brother for getting drunk, was a nuisance. Joyce loathed responsibility.

So where to go? He decided on Rome—the eternal city. It suited his destiny, or so he thought, and moreover his hero Ibsen had once wintered there. In truth the anger was whetting up in him, he was searching for that "fermented ink" to justify his bile in the same way as the shots of absinthe sizzled his brain. He was only twenty-four.

With the help of a letter that his father wheedled from the

Office of the Lord Mayor of Dublin four years previously Joyce secured a job as a bank clerk in Rome. Fortunately for him, a spendthrift, his duties did not consist of handing out folded wads of buff-colored lira; instead he was consigned to a back office writing business letters from eight-thirty in the morning until half past seven at night (with two hours off for lunch), sitting on an uncushioned scrawny straw-bottomed chair which tore his trousers. In the summer heat he wore a tailcoat to cover up this indecency. Dante may have been his spiritual food—the author in whom the spirit of the Renaissance was fully realized—but Rome was full of "black lice [Jesuits]." The ancient city—"ruins, piles of bones, and skeletons," Papal Rome resembling the slums of the Coombe in Dublin.

While the need for change and the mongrel creditors were his given reasons for leaving Trieste, he was unconsciously searching for a milieu that would bring him to a pitch of rage such as he had not known before. Even harsh memories of Dublin were tempered somewhat. He had been unfair to its hospitality, its ingenuous insularity and a natural beauty unequaled anywhere in Europe. He was reading Irish papers—*Sinn Féin* and *The Leprechaun*—immersing himself in political news and savoring the more notorious court cases. The most salacious and "a possible psychological peach" for future fiction was a divorce case involving an eighty-five-year-old Jewish jeweler, Morris Harris, who according to his young wife had treated her cruelly, carrying on an affair with his eighty-year-old housekeeper, committing indecent acts in the dining room, putting excrement in her nightgown and having sexual relations with little girls. As an afterthought Joyce noted that he had borrowed ten shillings from Harris's nephew at the time of his "hegira."

He identified with Jewishness, "the first race that wandered far over the earth," brothers in adversity to Joyce the wanderer. It wasn't only the Galilean who had suffered betrayal, James Joyce had had his Calvary. In another mood he identified with ancient Greece and sought, as he had Buck Mulligan say in *Ulysses*, to "Hellenize" Ireland. Greek "was the language of the mind." All that was required was a pen, an ink bottle and "fermented words" to write out those tiny little sentences concerning those who had betrayed him. Were his works to be only that, they would be temporal; his scroll is far deeper—he compassed body and soul, high and low, seemingly faithful to his secret conviction that literature is, in its essence, violence and desire. In this he is brother to John Webster.

Roman life proved intolerable. To Stanislaus enthroned once again as distant listener, he ridiculed his colleagues— balding bankers, politically asinine, who broke a lot of wind and complained about swellings in their anuses or their testicles. His dreaming life was no better—death, assassinations, and corpses. The shortage of money became more acute than it had been in Trieste for the simple reason that he was paid monthly and squandered his earnings in a matter of days. Then it was little sprees for Nora, Giorgio and himself—roast chicken, ham, bread, and a liter of wine; gifts for Nora, a tonic or a pair of gloves, and buoyed by these attentions she would revert to her old self and have him in stitches with her humor. "Is Jesus and God the same?" was one bit of sagacity, and the other was if the Ibsen he read was the Ibsen in the papers.

But soon again it was the old grind of their renting a room for just one night and Joyce giving a private lesson at the end of his long day to secure the next night's lodgings somewhere. A bambino was not welcome. That he managed to write and that she got through each listless day with her son is a tribute to both of them. But there were strains. His signature epiphanies were no longer the dreaming epithalamiums to her as opal and pearl; instead he described a drafty room, a weak-sighted poet and a small bed on which were seated a Madonna and a plaintive child. He said he would not be surprised if Nora did not unload a second male child to buttress the dynasty. As a precaution—and in vain—they slept head to foot. Nora became pregnant again.

The pattern of her life was even more crippling than his. At midday she would have to vacate the rented room and then with Giorgio wait in a café, or in a park, looking up at the rooftops or down at the river until her rescuer arrived with the money from the private lesson, their staple for the next twenty-four hours. If only she had kept a diary. Of what was she thinking? Loneliness? Disenchantment? Galway? A rainbow? She even delivered a complaining letter to him at his bank but all he could do was blow his nose in it. He noted also that her style, a marvel of illiteracy, would have perfectly fitted the sensibilities of Thomas Hardy's woebegone servant girls.

As a writer and dreamer he could imagine that which he did not have, but for her there were no such poetic ascensions and there was no money, no girlfriends, no chitter-chatter and no new clothes. He later expressed a memory of love's history as being "stars that burned with the pure though distant intensity." He was close to mental exhaustion. Any former ideas he had about socialism were abandoned. He was working in the bank, giving private tuitions, borrowing whenever he could and pestering his brother about his predicament. They had only four lire left to buy coal, lamp oil, candles and bread. It was impossible for him to write anything and yet somehow he did. He was conceiving the stories which would become *Dubliners*, luminous images of the city he professed to hate but which nevertheless are suffused with tenderness for those lost creatures "outcast from life's feast." His sense of the meticulous was already ingrained in him. For his story "Grace," in which there was a reference to the Pope's infallibility, he checked details by going to the Biblioteca Vittorio Emanuele to read the dogma of the proclamation and the names of the two dissenting clerics who, when they said "Non placet," got a "Kissmearse" dismissal from His Holiness—as Joyce put it in a letter to Stanislaus.

The bulletins to Stanislaus in Trieste were now frantic. If money did not come he was sunk. Stanislaus was to enclose it in good thick paper so that Joyce's employer at the bank— to whom he owed money—would not confiscate it. Sometimes the letters were plaintive. He had no pen, no ink, no paper, no peace, the family had had to do with pasta for their Christmas dinner. It seemed not to fret him unduly that Stanislaus had bread and ham in his bedroom for his Christmas dinner. Expenditures were myriad. Giorgio needed a new sheet for his bed and he broke windows and drinking vessels at will. Everything in Rome was conspiring against him. He was swindled in the tavern, Giorgio had accidentally received a lash of a horseman's whip under the eye, and Nora was in a fairly permanent state of gloom. His teeth were rotting and so was his soul. Life as he said was slipping from him like water from a muslin bag. Except that it wasn't. Here and despite everything, his intellectual rigor began to sizzle. "A keen regret" seized him if he did not arrive at an accurate understanding and appreciation of everything he encountered.

He would sit alone in a café at seven in the morning to go

over some of the phrases in his stories—"the rhythmic rise
and fall of words"; and of course to read. He was merciless in
his judgments. "Why are English novels so terribly boring," he
wrote and then went on to give a cruel though brilliant synop-
sis of a Hardy short story. Always beating about the bush English authors were. Irish authors did not fare much better—the
curlews-and-lakes school of thought! Oscar Wilde was not
tough-minded enough. The riot at the Abbey Theatre over
Synge's *Playboy of the Western World* excited him though he
had no sympathy for Synge. In the play Christy Mahon, the win-
some wooer, had spoken of "a dream of women standing in their
shifts," which the nationalist and religious motley deemed an
insult to Irish womanhood. For Joyce it merely demonstrated
the paucity of Synge's imagination. From his distant vantage
point, Joyce sided with the mob who had orchestrated the riots
in the theater each night because Synge had been accepted in
the fold of Yeats's literary clique and Joyce was not. The nation-
alists whom he glancingly admired at that time would later be
ridiculed too—"Intensities" gassing on about Vinegar Hill and
the lovely Irish gammon and spinach. French authors, he conceded, did have something to recommend them but their in-
flated sense of Gallic destiny was too much. Zola's vast history
of French mores he could not tackle and he questioned why
Verlaine had to be the future of Rimbaud. Only James Joyce
would be James Joyce's future.

All his life he was a voracious reader. He read books, pamphlets, manuals, street directories, everything and anything to
feed his eclectic tastes and his lust for knowledge. In his library after his death there were almost a thousand volumes,
books as diverse as *A Clue to the Creed of Early Egypt*, Apu-
leius, Aeschylus, *Psyche and Cupid*, Thomas Aquinas, Plato,

Nietzsche, Irish melodies, *Historic Graves of Glasnevin Cemetery*, Cowper's translation of the *Odyssey*, a pocket missal that had belonged to his cousin, Fanny Hill's unexpurgated memoirs, a book on uric acid, another on masturbation, a little handbook on fortune-telling by cards, and the catalogues from the modish shops in London and Dublin.

Without knowing it he had conceived of his novel *Ulysses*—"It is an epic of two races (Israelite-Irish) . . ."—and he had given voice to his daring manifesto. To Stanislaus he wrote that if he were to put a bucket down into his own soul's sexual department, he would also draw up the muddied waters of Arthur Griffith (leader of Sinn Féin), Ibsen, Saint Aloysius (his own saint name), Shelley and Renan, in short, cerebral sexuality and rank bodily fervor run amok. Not since the Jacobeans would sex be so openly and so rawly portrayed. Dickens, Thackeray, the Brontë sisters, Tolstoy, Flaubert, Proust, all had dwelt achingly on love, unrequited love, and by implication on sex, but Joyce was determined to break the taboos—to depict copulation, transvestism, onanism, coprophilia and all else that was repellent to Victorian England, puritanical America and sanctimonious Ireland. If people did not like it he couldn't help that either. On the "saince" of a certain subject, he said that very few mortals did not wake up each morning in dread of finding themselves syphilitic. "Talk about pure men, pure women and spiritual love" was all bunkum. There was no such thing. Sexuality was central to human impulse. More importantly sexuality was a universal trait and not just an Irish one—he would Hellenize, Hebrewize, demonize and immortalize his native city and for his crimes he would be punished and long after his death he would be rewarded by having snatches of his *Ulysses* transcribed on small bronze plaques and beveled into the pavements which Leopold Bloom and others had trodden.

The Holy Ghost as he put it was in the ink-bottle, "but the perverse devil of my literary conscience sitting on the hump of his pen."

The Roman "experiment" ended abruptly when, after a night's drinking, two hangers-on followed him outside, knocked him to the ground, stole the contents of his wallet then escorted him to a police station, pretending to be officers.

Stanislaus was to learn of it curtly. The telegram simply read—"arrive eight get room." Meeting them at the railway station, Stanislaus sensed without being told that there would soon be an addition to the family. Life became harsher. Joyce could not retrieve his old job at the school and had to hunt for new pupils. The hope of getting *Dubliners* published fell through once again. Wretched letters came from the family in Dublin. Sisters wrote to say that if there were any old clothes or a bit of money "it would be a Godsend." John Joyce painted a picture of a dismal Christmas and asked for even a pound from those "blackguard brothers," reminding them that he had not refused either of them when he had it. He was going into hospital soon and was certain that this would be his last request. Naturally, it wasn't.

It was James who was taken to hospital when he was struck down with rheumatic fever and soon after Nora was admitted to the pauper ward where Lucia was born. Nora said that she might have had the child in the street except that Stanislaus saved her. Joyce wanted the child named after the patron saint of eyes because of his occult fear of blindness. The family in Dublin did not approve. His sister Poppy wrote to say that their father thought Jim quite mad to pick an Italian name. Gogarty who was, by now, a qualified surgeon and practicing in Vienna, sent his barbed condolences regretting that Joyce would have so little time to recuperate. Six months, he insisted, were necessary "to ensure the safety of the cardiac valves." He also enclosed a pound to help them out. The pound never arrived. When Nora left the hospital she was given a charity gift of twenty crowns. Soon she was threatening to leave him again or punish him by having the children baptized. She would argue with him in Italian so as to exclude Stanislaus but when she wanted to reassert her connubial claims she might answer Joyce's question "Where will you meet me?" by saying "In bed, I suppose?"

These bickerings and reconciliations Stanislaus conveyed in letters to the solicitous Aunt Josephine who was full of sympathy for "poor Jim," predicting that Nora would not leave him, that her threats were all "my eye." It was "monstrous" to expect a genius like James Joyce to peel vegetables or mind the baby. She voiced her concern that there might be another child. Nora did conceive again but lost it and Joyce with his morbid curiosity said that he was the only one in the household who had dwelt on that truncated fetus and mourned it. Aunt Josephine, otherwise averse to drink, sympathized with Joyce's inordinate drinking, said it was on account of the many rebuffs he had had over *Dubliners* and that as with any man he drank "to find forgetfulness." Throughout it all, Joyce had managed to give public lectures and had begun to transform the 914-page outpourings of *Stephen Hero* into the perfect distillation of *A Portrait of the Artist as a Young Man*, after he completed his great short story "The Dead" in 1907.

In 1909, he decided that it was time his family in Ireland met his little son and he proposed sending the boy home along with Stanislaus. Sensing in their reply some reserve, he decided that he himself was not welcome and neither was the child because of his illegitimacy. No words of appeasement would satisfy. He would go himself. The hidden reasons were far more reverberative. He had to suffer once again at the hands of his brethren.

Betrayal

IN *ULYSSES* STEPHEN SAYS: "A man of genius makes no mistakes." He was right. Dublin was waiting to discharge more wrongs on his already scalding psyche and the three visits which he made between 1909 and 1912 led to such emotional havoc that he broke with his native city forever.

On that first visit home he was to be told of a betrayal which convulsed him with grief and was soon to be followed by a renewed delirium for Nora's body. The arrival with Giorgio was not propitious. He was a superstitious man and sighting Oliver Gogarty's "fat back" on the platform at Kingstown boded ill. His father and his sisters were there to greet the prodigal son and to partially forgive him for having eloped. His father had written to him about the terrible mistake he had made by leaving with Miss Barnacle, crushing not only a father's feelings but thwarting a life of promise "in one blasted breath." The sight of a little boy and "a more melancholy James" melted them and drew exclamations from the sisters about his being too foreign-looking.

That week James and John patched up their differences, or seemed to. They decided to leave the house full of women and take a walk up the Dublin Mountains. It entailed a tram journey to Ticknock and to brace themselves for the climb they slipped into the Yellow House for a few chasers. Buoyed by drink, John began to sing and by way of forgiving his son, accompanied himself on the piano with a moment from *La Traviata*—"My soul is too eaten by remorse. . . . Ah! Foolish old man! Only now I see the harm I did." Through his tears he asked James why he had ever gone and left him. To that there was no answer, but parents are parents, and Irish parents the most solicitous of all.

As one breach was mended, another was ready to open up. Secrets would spew out that brought him to the pitch of derangement. Gogarty, determined not to be slighted, pursued his old friend and with customary ribaldry declared him a mess— "Jaysus, man, you're in phthisis." Joyce remained aloof, refused to engage in the banter and, as he told Stanislaus, refused grog, wine, coffee and tea. He also mentioned that Dublin rumor had it that Synge died of syphilis. It is astonishing how pitiless Joyce could be about others, yet when adversity struck at his own door he railed. The first outcry came one early morning by telegram when he announced to Nora, "I am not going to Galway nor is Giorgio."

He who had such a burning need to be betrayed was to get his fill of it. At the time that she used to meet him she had on alternate nights stood with another, put an arm around him and lifted her face to be kissed. He did not even name that other, each knowing that of course he meant Vincent Cosgrave, "the Rum Rooster." Since their elopement, whenever Nora wanted to hurt Joyce she would tell him that Cosgrave thought him mad. Between them Gogarty and Cosgrave had hatched a plot. For different reasons they wanted to be avenged on Joyce. Cosgrave had failed in his wooing of Nora and he was being parodied in Joyce's autobiographical novel as "lynxeyed Lynch," a man of "excrementitious intelligence," who upon listening to

Stephen's theories of beauty, deemed them "true scholastic stink."

Joyce had been imprudent enough to allow chapters of his work to circulate in Dublin. His vow of abstinence did not last long and soon he was drinking with Cosgrave, rakes together as in the old days. Then one afternoon Cosgrave struck. Nora had gone out with him too, they had walked along the canal and out to Ringsend; in short Joyce had been deceived. A cuckold. Accusations shot across the Irish Sea. His eyes were full of tears, his heart full of bitterness, he was wounded, dishonored, destroyed for all time. His faith in her was broken. He would leave for Trieste immediately, once Stanislaus had procured the fare money. All was over between them. At the same time, he was begging her to write to tell him if the hand that touched him in the dark and the voice that spoke to him in the dark was gone forever. Had she walked the same streets, lingered on the banks of the Dodder and dispensed her soft favors to this other? And what else, what else? Though his faith in her was broken he was nevertheless soliciting pity for his poor mistaken wretched love. For the sake of that wretched love, she was to write to him by return. Was Giorgio his son? Were not the bloodstains in the Hope guest house in Zurich that first time a little slight? He wallowed in his own wretchedness and thought that probably parading "his son" in Dublin had made him an object of ridicule. He called on his last-remaining friend, J. F. Byrne, who lived at No. 7 Eccles Street, an address to be made famous in *Ulysses*, and poured out the grievances of tortured soul and tortured body. Byrne assured him that it was a damn lie, Cosgrave and Gogarty had hatched the plot to break him. They were jealous because of Nora but more so, because of a sneaking certainty that maybe he had the makings of a poet, that maybe his private aesthetic, "a thoughtenchanted silence," would crown him Ireland's Homer after all.

Back in Trieste, Nora enlisted Stanislaus's help as she read those craven and lunatic bulletins. Stanislaus was able to assure her and then James that Cosgrave had always wanted to get "inside" Nora over Joyce. Recantation followed. How could he have doubted her? What a worthless fellow he was. What a sweet noble creature she was. He sent three bags of shell cocoa to fatten her up for his joyous homecoming. So it was back to the swooning declarations, "the deeps of her heart," the "soft rose-like joy of her love," the strange uncertain reveries with which it filled him. They would fight the foul plot and never mistrust one another again. He gloried in describing a gift he had got for her, a necklace of ivory dice on a gold-fetter chain and in the central tablet a declaration—"Love is unhappy when love is away." Each letter now brimming with hope and promise. He would make tons of money. He would never use coarse words in her company again. He was even being accepted in Dublin. In the bar of the Gresham Hotel he heard his countrymen call him "the poet of my race" and with that laurel and Nora's love they were about to enter the "heaven of our life" on no money. He managed to get a first-class pass (to London only) on account of being a member of the Italian press corps and in his newly found expansiveness, he decided to bring his sister Eva to join the family in Trieste. At the very same time his telegram to Stanislaus read, "[Arriving] Tomorrow at eight. Penniless."

Penniless or not, he had accrued some formidable experience. The crazed jealousy had reignited his passionate love for Nora and once again her body became "musical and strange and perfumed." The fact that she neither confirmed nor denied the trysts with Cosgrave inflamed his desire as he tasted in his imagination the nectar of the voyeur. Whether it was true or not, it would become true for literature. He conceived the plot for his play *Exiles* in which husband and best friend would vie for a woman's love, the husband admitting that in "some terrible part of his ignoble being" he longed to be betrayed by her.

Nora's powers over him were strengthened. She had proved herself the stronger one, he, the suitor, asking that their future love be "fierce and violent."

Many have been baffled that a man of Joyce's daunting intellect chose and remained constant to this peasant woman. It is beyond these letters, it is beyond propriety, it remains inexplicable as the Eleusinian mysteries.

Buckets

"FOR ME it will always be the first city in the world," he said of Dublin. It is inconceivable to think that he is not buried there.

An attempt was made by Samuel Beckett and other friends in 1958, a venture which failed because of Irish religiosity and Swiss bureaucracy, two intractable institutions. A firm of Dublin undertakers recoiled at the thought of handling the unclean remains.

Eva, homesick for Dublin, used to complain that the only saving grace about Trieste was its cinema house. To a man hounded by debts, this was nothing short of a windfall. He would go into business.

He was not the first writer hoping to make money by some means other than the pen. Balzac had done the same, his folly—though not his genius—commensurate with Joyce's. Balzac thought of owning a newspaper and borrowed thirty thousand francs to revive a moribund one. For his pains he went to jail where he insisted that his servant come in livery, bringing flowers, a woman's lock of hair and whatever fruits were in season. His cell was carpeted and fitted with Belgian lace shawls, mirrors and a divan on which he hoped to seduce his personable female visitors.

Joyce found four businessmen who ran a group of theaters

in the city and a cinema called the Cinematograph Volta in Bucharest and persuaded them to become his partners. They would open a cinema not only in Dublin but also in Cork and Belfast and all that was needed was his fare, his fervor, and ten crowns per day for his food and board.

Once back in Dublin he threw himself into the enterprise, found a vacant premises in Mary Street, had it wired and fitted with seats and chose a trio of pictures which were bound to generate tender sentiments in his native city. They were *The First Paris Orphanage*, *La Pourponnière* and *The Tragic Story of Beatrice Cenci*, all of which would be enhanced by a little string orchestra.

It was in his father's house in Fontenoy Street, his glands in a pandemonium, that he received the cue from Nora. Baldly, she had written to say that she wished to be fucked by him. Night after night, his prick was kept hot from the brutal imaginary drives which he gave her. The bucket had to be sent down into a woman's sexual department to know her at her most torrid and who best to meet his summons than Nora, she who had "made him a man" that first night in Ringsend. Just as Leopold Bloom would wallow in the inner organs of beast and fowls, Joyce wanted to wallow in the inner maelstrom of woman's desire. No longer the self-pitying or exalted paeans about knocking at the door of her heart, it was now body calling to body, his flinging her down on that soft belly of hers and ripping her white drawers. She was his lust-mad accomplice "with the whore's glow in her slumbrous eyes." Their hectic copulations had to be relived in order to further their rabid desires and to substantiate his leap in literature.

Nora had initiated this scalding marathon, either in a moment of extreme desire or in a determination to keep him excited and faithful to her in his absence. She was in Trieste with two small children, his sister Eva, and Stanislaus who had been delegated to take over some of Joyce's teaching duties. While the cinema plans consumed him in the day, a rabid lust possessed him at night. Past couplings were graphically dwelt on and sustained as only memory sustains and invigorates reality. "Touch has a memory," Baudelaire said and for Joyce, in his father's house, every detail of his wife's body, bubbies, cunt, and spluttering tongue were described back to her at near orgasmic pitch. In the "secret sinful night" he sat at the kitchen table, frigging himself, knowing that she was either reading a letter he had sent or composing one of her own repeating the word which had set him off—"brief, brutal, irresistible and devilish."

He challenged her not only to match the hog in him but to surpass him on the altar of degradation and depravity. "Dirtier and dirtier" was the password, his "dirty red lumpy pole" going into her "rank red cunt," his "cockstand tearing through a slit in her drawers." He gave back to her her wild capitulations, the splutter of foul words, her peal of farts, every raw and shaming moment for which he loved her even more. Occasionally there was a reference to her as being still his queen, his "beautiful wildflower," but the thrust of his incantations lay in recalling past ecstasies and envisaging future ones. He reminded her of the first night in Ringsend when her long tickly fingers frigged him slowly until he came, gazing at him with saintlike eyes, and in the Zurich guest house willing him to be larger, longer, sturdier, riotously heckling him to "Fuck up, love! Fuck up, love!" Did she do the same for Cosgrave, his rival and the man whose heart he longed to stop with the click of a revolver? She must tell him so. No last secret must remain between them and even if every lout in Galway had had her before he met her, it now only quickened his desires.

The very sight of her handwriting, her disjointed words kissed and held to the secret parts of her body kept him agog for a whole day until their night communiqués. She was depicted in different roles, a stern creature summoning him into a room to reprimand him and there seated on a chair, her fat thighs apart, a cane in her hand about to flog him. Flog. Flog. He would be grateful if she would also fuck him dressed in full outdoor costume with hat and veil, her boots muddy as she straddled him. Frilly drawers and Molly Bloom's luxuriated-on, crimson flower completed the tableau. The envisaged couplings were to be enacted in every quarter of their apartment, the well of the stairs and the dark closet, their rutting hole. He craved to hear the dirty words and the dirty stories which other girls had told her. But he also craved redemption. She was to fuck all she could out of him for the first few nights in order that he be cured. He, the weaker one, small and soft, a creature whom no other girl in Europe would waste her time on. He assures her that he will not go to the whores again.

She writes that she is going without underwear because of these hot solicitations. He revels in it, orders her to take herself to some secret corner of the apartment and tickle her little cocky, so as to write more vividly, to underline the words and to hold them to her person. Then a note of caution. He is afraid she will give herself to somebody. If that somebody were Stanislaus, who was sleeping only a wall away and who was himself attracted to Nora, then Joyce would have found the ultimate betrayal which he zealously sought.

As the days and nights passed, the dirty words and the dirt-

ier deeds began to show traces of exhaustion. Lecherous vow-
ings were tempered now with bouts of sentiment. He had gone
to the hotel where she had worked and had asked a maid to be
allowed up to her bedroom where he abandoned himself to an
orgy of tears and longed to kneel and pray as the Three Kings
from the East had prayed before the manger in which Jesus
lay. His letters ran the whole gamut, from consuming lust to
resurrected love, then predictable moments of domesticity. He
would like some new brown linoleum for their kitchen floor, red
curtains and an armchair so that he, "the knight of the rueful countenance," could sit and talk and talk with "the little
mother" who would take him into the dark sanctuary of her
womb.

Having assured Stanislaus that they would make tons of
money, he was once again imploring his brother to save the
family from eviction at all costs. The cinema venture did not
succeed, partly because of inclement weather, the lugubrious
choice of films, and disenchantment on the part of the four
businessmen who, having sunk sixteen hundred pounds in the
project, packed their bags and went home. Meanwhile his
family in Trieste were faced with eviction. He hit on two other
deluded schemes—to import skyrockets into Trieste and to
serve as an agent for Donegal tweeds. They came to nothing
and so while relaying his glandular excesses to Nora, he was
once again asking Stanislaus to save the family from eviction at
"all costs."

Much has been written about the impropriety of publishing
the infamous letters and Richard Ellmann, who selected them,
was castigated. Years earlier far less incriminating ones were
published with the permission of Nora and George, and Samuel
Beckett fumed against literary widows, saying that they should

be "burned on a pyre along with the writer himself." But do they make us think any less of Joyce or of Nora? Do they demean the marriage? Hardly. True, they are as outright in their earthiness as the mystics are in their ecstasies, yet they share the mystic's longing for a couple to dissolve into one. Joyce's chaos is our chaos, his barbaric desires are ours too, and his genius is that he made such breathless transcendations out of torrid stuff, that from the mire he managed to "bestir the hearts of men and angels." Moreover he was a young man filled with a scalding passion and at that very same time attending a hospital in Dublin to be treated for a "damned dirty complaint," an infection which he had picked up from a prostitute.

These letters are about more than smut. First and foremost they are a measure of the inordinate trust that he had in Nora to allow him to be all things, the child-man, the man-child, the peeping Tom, and the grand seducer. But there is also her own sexual prowess, no small thing for a convent girl from Galway and a radical thing in defiance of that male collusion whereby women are expected to maintain a mystique and conceal their deepest sexual impulses. Sexuality and maternity being thought to be contrary.

The letters are fascinating for yet another reason—why did he never destroy them or ask her to destroy them? He who was so obsessed with secrecy that he would not allow even his sisters to see Nora's underclothes when they had come back from the wash, was sending these ejaculations into a small apartment where any member of the family could easily have chanced upon them. He was also asking Nora to conceal her excitement, almost. Almost! The voyeur in him had at last been unleashed and in his own city, amongst his own kin and in the country which he believed had repressed him and upon which he wished to pour the glorious and unabated bucket of sexual slime. The letters were for Nora, of course, but they were also for Joyce, to convince himself that he was free of every vestige of Roman Catholic guilt. But was he?

In 1928 H. G. Wells, who would not have known of these letters, wrote to Joyce: "You really believe in chastity, purity and the personal God and that is why you are always breaking out in cries of cunt, shit, and hell." Wells may have been right but Joyce had committed his most secret impulses to paper both as testament and liberation. He had put the buckets down, man's and woman's, and while his prose would still shimmer with the tender arrestingness of "Would one but to do apart a lilybit her virginelles," there would come Molly Bloom's "amplitudinously curvilinear" spiel and the rapture of Issy in *Finnegans Wake*, "rising up in the twilight, after the grandest goosegreasing of all from Mick, Nick the Maggot," one of the monks who had transcribed the Gospels into Irish.

He did not offer these letters to the world but neither did he ensure that they be destroyed. In 1940, when they were leaving Paris, Nora did burn his letters to her because, as she told Helen Nutting, "They were nobody else's business." But Shem the Penman was of a different predilection. His omission has pre-echoes of Earwicker, that "duddurty devil" who wanted to make his private linen public after he "thried to two in the Fiendish park," the secret left intact to flutter across Ireland on a clean white handkerchief, or a clean white page. Now there's the rub.

Obstacles

"I DO NOT WANT to be a literary Jesus Christ," he said. Want it or not, it became his lot. The short stories which he began writing when he was twenty-two, did not find a publisher until he was thirty-two and had in all done the rounds of numerous publishing houses. When he was asked by George Russell to submit to *The Irish Homestead* stories of a simple, moral, pathetic nature for which he was guaranteed a payment of a sovereign, he was already in revolt.

The first story was "The Sisters" and two others followed that caused umbrage about his depiction of Irish life and the Irish character. Readers did not like to be ridiculed and pilloried in this way. Joyce himself admitted that a sense of mischief often took him over when he put pen to paper but he also insisted that he was trying to get his fellow countrymen to have one good look at themselves in his "nicely polished looking-glass."

The collected stories he called *Dubliners* and in 1906 Grant Richards, an English publisher, signed a contract for them. The "funferal" was about to commence. The printer took exception to the questionable material. Offending phrases were as shocking as "bloody" or a woman who "changed the position of her legs often."

"O one-eyed printer!" Joyce railed, insisting that he was not going to prostitute himself, he was not prepared to change a word. In less heated exchanges he urged Richards to be active initiating alterations in English taste. The printer, fearing prosecution, bowed out and Richards followed suit. After trying several other publishers Joyce met his nemesis, a Dubliner, George Roberts, whom he had known since his youth. Earlier objections seemed incidental compared with what was to come.

If Keats according to his own admission was half in love with easeful death, Joyce was more than half in love with persecution. His experience with Roberts is a catalogue of prevarication, ignorance and yobbery. Having said he would publish the stories Roberts and his stalwart printer, a Mr. Falkner, began to sniff danger. Joyce was unrelenting. He said he was not to be blamed for the odor of ash pits and rotted cabbage and offal in these stories because that was how he saw his city. "We are foolish, comic, motionless, corrupted, yet we are worthy of sympathy too," he said haughtily and added that if Ireland were to deny that sympathy to its characters, the rest of the world would not. In this he was mistaken.

Each story, like each "unhappy family," was offensive in a different way. In "Ivy Day in the Committee Room" King Edward VII is referred to as being "an ordinary knockabout" and a man "fond of his glass of grog." Roberts thought this libelous and having tried every avenue of suave persuasion Joyce eventually wrote to King George V, asking him to give his blessing to the offending paragraph. Not surprisingly, a matter-of-fact reply came back through a secretary, saying that it was inconsistent with royal protocol for His Majesty to express an opinion on such matters. Joyce agreed to the cuts but true to his scalding nature he wrote to the Irish newspapers about this bastardization of his art, something which did not endear him to Roberts or his cohorts.

"Our experiences seek us out because we want them to," Richard Ellmann says in his essay on Joyce and Consciousness. Certainly the saga of *Dubliners* and other Joycean feuds bear that out. No sooner had he agreed to cuts in one story than Roberts came thundering in with another. Joyce called on his literary friends in vain. Thomas Kettle read the stories and said they would do harm to Ireland. With each passing day, qualm and objection intensified. The stories were anti-Irish, a sentiment which ran counter to Roberts' aim as a patriotic publisher. The mention of various public houses would encourage every publican to sue. Joyce, who had sped to Dublin to expedite matters, suggested that he and Roberts call on each publican to get an undertaking that they would not sue. Had this pub crawl taken place, it would have formed the ribald matter for columns by Myles na Gopaleen, a brilliant Irish columnist and writer. Myles, himself no stranger to drink, insisted that Joyce was alive and well and working in a pub on the road to Mullingar.

Joyce was obliged to engage a solicitor in order to sway Roberts. Unfortunately the solicitor he chose, George Lidwell, had more experience in acting for police complaints than in the niceties of fiction. Far from being an ally, he was to prove subversive. He found the language questionable in every story but most hideous of all was the story "An Encounter" in which the loathsome subject that dare not speak its name had found a voice. This was the hint of homosexuality at the end of the story where an old codger who has waylaid two young boys revels in the pleasures of flogging, then moves away to do something

which shocks them. Mr. Lidwell, who had some glancing acquaintance with Gibbons, fumed about this vice "of which
modesty rejects the name and nature abominates the idea." So
Joyce was now at war with three institutions, the rock of Rome,
the English Crown and the legal profession. Seeing that recal-
citrance was getting him nowhere he changed tactics; he
became conciliatory, even mendacious. He would delete this
paragraph, that paragraph, he would even remove the abomina-
ble story, but with each concession came a new demand. Then
for him, "the most unkindest cut of all." Thomas Kettle vowed
that he would slate that book because of its homosexual element. Kettle was a literary man and an idealist who in the spirit
of young Fortinbras enlisted to fight in the First World War, yet
any smear or imagined smear on his countrymen incensed him.
Joyce was isolated. Even his own father thought he must be a
ruffian to have written that stuff. To Nora who was in Galway
with the children he wrote of his desperation, lamenting that
the child which he had carried in the womb of his imagination
for so many years would never be born. She sent a telegram
telling him not to give up hope. Encouraged by this, he plans
for her to come to Dublin for the Horse Show and hopes to be
able to buy her some new hats.

Roberts then came up with a bogus solution. Joyce could
write a preface in the form of an apology. Joyce, good at the
demur, promised to think about it and went to Galway believing
he could outwit his enemy. To an outsider, and certainly in retrospect, Roberts did not really want to publish *Dubliners* but
neither was he willing to let it go. In his balking unconscious
way he wanted to crucify Joyce. To Galway further doubts were
dispatched. Roberts could foresee libel actions and seismic
moral indignation. The Lord Lieutenant's wife, Lady Aberdeen,

a stalwart of the Dublin vigilante committee, would be shocked, as would the entire country, and Roberts' own fiancée would undoubtedly jilt him.

Joyce hastened to Dublin, pawned his watch and chain, and searched out a fellow writer Padraic Colum to accompany him to Roberts's office to plead. It did not go well—argument, counterargument and vindication got so heated that the two writers were asked to leave. Joyce now pinned all hopes on Lidwell and entertained him in the Ormond Hotel to sweeten matters. Lidwell would write a less incriminating letter about the stories and the problem would be solved. The crafty Roberts refused to read the letter because it had been addressed to Joyce and not to him and Lidwell, himself no stranger to trickery, said he could not write to Roberts because he was not a client of his. At the very same time Joyce's brother Stanislaus was writing from Trieste to say that the Joyce family had been ordered to vacate their flat in nine days because of defecting on their rent. Joyce in cavalier mood told his brother not to worry about this problem as he would hire a lawyer in Trieste and fight a legal case with his landlord. Joyce the great man for the lampooning pamphlets was soon becoming the great would-be litigator.

Things had reached stasis. Roberts would only publish if Joyce signed an agreement to pay for the cost of the first edition if books were seized. He suggested two securities of a thousand pounds each, as remote to Joyce as his pawned watch was. Emboldened now with his brilliant strategies, Roberts produced a letter which had come from a firm of solicitors in London advising him that because of the names of shops, public houses and railway companies, Joyce had broken his contract by submitting a libelous book. Lidwell had by then vanished and Joyce had hired another solicitor, a Mr. Dixon, who having read the stories fumed and attacked Joyce for squandering his talent and disgracing his country. Warming to the blood sport, Roberts came up with his ultimate ruse—he would sell Joyce the printed sheets for thirty pounds and Joyce could have the book printed in England. Promising to think it over Joyce left the office, with miraculously one set of proofs in his keeping, and within twenty-four hours the printer Mr. Falconer, in an orgy of righteousness, told Roberts that he would not take the money for printing the stories and moreover he was about to destroy them. He did. Roberts with a schoolboy's glee told Joyce that the stories had been destroyed "by guillotining and pulping." The execution was complete.

That evening Joyce sat in his Aunt Josephine's house playing a love song on the piano and weeping. His aunt asked Nora to go up and comfort him because the tears were for her too and for wearied love.

Next day the Joyces left "Moy Eireann" forever.

His parting volley was a broadsheet written on the train journey between Munich and Trieste in which he imagined Roberts' bilious reasoning.

Gas from a Burner

Shite and onions Do you think I'll print
The name of the Wellington Monument
Sydney Parade and Sandymount tram
Downes's cakeshop and Williams's jam. . . .

I'll burn that book so help me devil.
I'll sing a psalm as I watch it burn
And the ashes I'll keep in a one-handled urn.

James Joyce

> I'll penance do with farts and groans
> Kneeling upon my marrowbones.
> This very next lent I will unbare
> My penitent buttocks to the air.

His unemployed brother Charlie had the dubious pleasure of circulating this throughout Dublin.

Two years later, the original publisher Grant Richards, deeming the moral climate less stringent, decided to publish *Dubliners*. The reviews were mixed, the material thought to be drab and morbid, the author accused of dealing with subjects not normally aired. One year later 379 copies had been sold, 120 of which were purchased somehow, by the impecunious James Joyce.

Dalliance

"I WILL NEVER leave you again," he wrote to Nora during one of his visits to Dublin. He never did leave her but in his thirties he underwent "the kinchite quiver" on three occasions. Just as the imagination has to be rescued from abstraction so too has the hunger for a new and romantic love. For all his scathingness, and despite his unremitting intellect, Mr. Joyce was a romantic when it came to women. Bed her, red her, and tread her was for his fictions; in life he had said, "First we feel. Then we fall." One of his falls was for a woman in Locarno where he had gone to recover from an eye operation. She was a young doctor, Gertrude Kaempffer, recovering from tuberculosis, a wounded soul like himself. He wrote her passionate letters that were wildly inappropriate. He wished her to see into his soul, as he did with Nora, but he wanted this stranger to also know of his first sexual arousal when a nursemaid told him to turn away while she urinated. Miss Kaempffer understandably thought such confidences somewhat precipitate and resolutely avoided him. Her genteel excuse was that their friendship might hurt his wife.

Another conquest was a little more successful for the very simple reason that it was one of his students, Amalia Popper, a young girl with eyes like an antelope and a happy singsong voice. She was the daughter of a Jewish merchant named

Leopoldo and Joyce, believing that he himself was Jewish in the "bowels," thought the attraction had ancestral and mystical connotations. He would arrive for a lesson wearing his father's old yellow waistcoat, then loll on two chairs, puffing away and encouraging puns:

> Mephistopheles = Mavis Toffeelips
> Xmas cake = chrissormiss wake
> De Profundis = deepbrow fundigs

They liked this eccentricity. They could tease him about a ring he wore which was a talisman against blindness just as they could scold him for not wearing a wedding ring. Subjects varied according to his whims. "Generally" was to be pronounced like General Li, a Chinese warrior who hanged himself, and this would lead to a long discourse on Chinese autocracy. He charmed and unnerved them by turn, painting word pictures of each one. A girl might for instance be a rose garden full of birds and flowers but on closer inspection be a heap of coal. Another might be very ladylike until she slipped on the street. He was slipping himself. He sang for them, he sang "Dooleysprudence" but he was losing his own. Amalia held his blood in thrall. Her bewitchment of him was later converted into a crystalline prose poem, *Giacomo Joyce*. She was a veiled girl, frail as web, a Semite in odorous furs.

Home life consisted of duties, two young children, Nora making sporadic threats to leave him and a constant scraping for money. By contrast, Amalia represented Gothic grandeur, ensconced as she was in her ancient castle, coats of mail on the wall, her high heels clacking on the stone stairs and himself wanting a word with her ladyship. His thoughts of her were half worshipful, half caustic: she was pictured in a rice field of Vercelli, smiling a false smile, rancid yellow humor lurking within the softened pulp of her eyes. He sensed a needly venom in her velvet iris. She was his Hedda! Hedda Gabler. It was chiefly a love affair of the eyes. The difference in age, her decorousness and the bourgeois insulation of her life made for one kind of barrier but so did his own troubled conscience—"Easy now, Jamesy! Did you never walk the streets of Dublin at night sobbing another name?"

Her father's influence over her he stipulated in a lecture which he gave on *Hamlet* and which he insisted she attend. Prating Polonius and a canny wary Leopoldo Popper were merged. When, soon after, he was told at the door of her house that she had been taken to hospital with appendicitis he walked away distraught. The virginal body being gashed by the surgeon's knife, the beautiful antelope eyes filled with suffering. She recovered but he was soon to detect a wintry expression in her smile. She began to avert her eyes and the day he was dismissed from teaching her he thought that the piano in her apartment resembled a coffin. It was not only the end of an unconsummated affair, it was the end of youth, and in *Giacomo Joyce* the benighted narrator says: "the end is here. It will never be." She would be material for fiction—"Write it, damn you, write it! What else are you good for?"

The next "fall" was for a "Marthe," Marthe Fleischmann, an aristocratic beauty who was kept by a wealthy engineer Rudolf Hiltpold in an apartment quite close to where Joyce lived in Zurich. A lady of leisure who smoked, put rosewater handkerchiefs in her cleavage and read novelettes as Molly Bloom would. She must have felt confounded by this new and overexcitable suitor. One account tells us that upon seeing her going in her own doorway he gasped and told her how she reminded him of a girl he saw years before in Dublin wading out to sea—his future Nausikaa. He plied her with letters even before he knew her name. Having handed them in at her apartment, he would then stand on the street outside and watch her read. She must have been puzzled and probably was flattered by such fretful, high-flown, operatic paeans. He hoped she was Jewish, a pagan Mary. His Irish Mary was at home resenting housework. He begged for a letter back, uncustomarily invoking God's aid. These bulletins were in German and French and for fear of being discovered he made a halfhearted attempt at disguising his handwriting. She was a pretty little animal with waving feathers, there was something frank and shameless about her despite her hauteur. No longer the arrogant young man who had scarified his colleagues in Dublin, he was now the supplicant—a poor seeker in the world waiting for her, visualizing her coming toward him in black, young, strange and gentle. Reams of sexual longing and dizzying self-absorption. Lest she feel too exhausted or too nervous to write he would send a self-addressed envelope to make things easier. A word would suffice. A yes, a no. Was she suffering as he was? Was she out of her mind? Certainly he was when he told her that he looked at the paper each morning fearing to read her name in the death announcements. His wife did not know and had she, there would be ructions. Years later she flew indignant when he was photographed with a fashionable hostess who claimed that her bedside reading was *Ulysses*. He would like to send his Martha flowers but was afraid. The secret might be discovered. He sent her a copy of his poems *Chamber Music* and then stood outside the window watching her read these notations of his soul. She was his "O rosa mistica, ora pro me!"

She agreed to meet him. Always a great one for the anniver-

saries he chose to entertain her on his birthday—February 2—
which was also Candlemas Day. The rendezvous was to be in
Frank Budgen's apartment. Budgen, who liked Nora, was reluc-
tant about this but relented when Joyce told him that it was es-
sential to his spiritual and artistic development. He got there
early, carrying a Jewish candlestick which he had borrowed
from an antique dealer. Asked what it was for he replied that it
was "for a black mass."

On Budgen's wall there were prints which seemed a little
too muted and not the stuff of conquest. He insisted that Budgen dash off a few charcoal nudes and that done, he had to vacate his own apartment, promising to rejoin Joyce with wife and
children for a late birthday party. By nightfall everything was
ready. He had lit the candles both because they were romantic
and because he wished to be able to see his visitor in a flatter-
ing light. His pagan Mary both yielded and withheld. He confided to Budgen when they met later on that he had "explored
the coldest and hottest parts of a woman's body." Fathom that!
A Martha in life, she would duplicate as a Martha in fiction but
with some of the traits of Molly Bloom. When her jealous patron
discovered her misdemeanor Joyce was summoned to the
apartment and not being of Pushkin's temperament he apologized, lamented the weakness in the male and promised that he
would not see her again.

In *The Book as World* the author Marilyn French says that
"it seems certain that Joyce had a contempt for women." It
doesn't; in his thoughts just as in his works, everything about
him was both complex and paradoxical. He agreed with Blake
for choosing a woman of "hazy and sensual disposition" but
recognized that Blake, like himself, out of a sublime egotism
wanted to fashion the woman into a creation of his own. As a

young man he could be quite outspoken and Stanislaus tells us that James would guess as to which woman was warmest between the thighs "to give a fella a great push." He liked to quote a clinical homily of the time in which woman was depicted simply as an animal who micturates once a day, defecates once a week, menstruates once a month, and parturates once a year. A long way that from "a woman to her lover clings the more the more."

Like any great artist Joyce had radical and shifting thoughts about everything. In an article about *A Doll's House* he said that Ibsen had dealt with the most important revolution possible, the relationship between men and women. Concurrently he was saying that Irishwomen were the cause of all moral suicide. The marriage of Socrates and Xanthippe he commended only because it helped Socrates to perfect the art of the dialectic, having to contend with a shrew. Yet he claimed that a man who had not lived daily with a woman was in his opinion incomplete. He cited Jesus, Faust and Hamlet as being lacking for this very reason.

In his early fiction the women were sacrificial creatures modeled on the women around him, the mothers and the sisters socially and economically beholden to the men whom they served. Worn out with childbearing, child rearing, and the washing of corpses, they believed that they were securing divine mercy for the next world.

A young girl in his story "Eveline" is about to go away on the boat with a young man but at the last moment has her doubts. Hearing the street organs and the plash of the water she draws back with a "No! No! No!" her white face passive, her eyes giving no sign of love, farewell, or recognition. With "All the seas of the world tumbled about her heart" she decides to return to take care of her father. In fact Joyce empathized with women far more than with men. "A Painful Case," written when he was in his early twenties, tells of the unfortunate Mrs. Emily Sinico who became attracted to a Mr. Duffy, a man who "abhorred anything which betokened physical or mental disorder." Mrs. Sinico urged him to let his nature open to the full and became his confessor until the day or the night when she unwisely pressed his hand to her face. It was too much for the reclusive bachelor. He broke off the relationship forever. Four years later when he read a small announcement of her death in an evening paper he was filled with revulsion for her vice. Her daughter had confessed at the inquest that her mother was in the habit of going out late at night to buy spirits and thus met her death crossing the railway line. As the story ends, Mr. Duffy's revulsion is replaced by a pang of conscience as to why he had killed her. In all the stories the women, despite being victims, attain a moral superiority. They are nobler than the men who have dominated them. In "The Dead," Gabriel Conroy watches his wife asleep and realizes how marginal his place is in her life since her dead lover inhabits her dreams.

In the more aesthetic *A Portrait of the Artist* women were idealized creatures, seabirds with raised skirts wading out to sea in a childlike innocence, but once he met Nora Barnacle his women were to embody the ethereal and the sexual. No longer victims, they developed into temptresses and sorceresses. In *Ulysses* they are masters of cunning and of charm. Gerty MacDowell on Sandymount strand, her yellow flower punishing Leopold Bloom's man flower, was a mere prologue to the appetites of Molly Bloom, a woman exceeding all habits and hungers. Vladimir Nabokov wrote of Molly's triteness and vulgarity and wished for a sharp pencil to separate those torrential sentences of hers. Her author saw it differently. He kept a photo of a Greek statue on his desk to keep himself engrossed in this creation whose cardinal points were breasts, arse, womb and cunt. He admitted that it was more obscene than anything else he had written but added that she was also "perfectly sane full amoral fertilizable untrustworthy engaging prudent indifferent." Molly's credo was "Let's have a bit of fun first." Indifferent to politics ("them Sinner Fein") she dilates on each and every aspect of life, conjures up sexual adventures even though her lover Blazes Boylan ("Doesn't know poetry from a cabbage") has already visited her that very day and muses on her husband moseying about, gazing at women, at their gluey lips and their finery, then home with a cock and a bull story, but she with eyes in the back of her head knows that he "came somewhere." She concludes that love it is not or he'd be off his feed. Only Chaucer's Wife of Bath can rival Molly in her frank and wildly humorous evaluation of men.

In her book *Sexual Politics* Kate Millett said that Joyce "engaged in the naïve participation in the cult of the primitive woman." There is nothing naïve in Joyce and if he depicted women as sexually primitive he was more prescient than anyone before or since. In fact he was far more indulgent of women than of men and he had reason to be, what with Nora, Sylvia Beach, Harriet Weaver—a trio providing inspiration, publication and patronage. He trusted women far more than he trusted men. He said relationships between men were founded on competitiveness, jealousy, rivalry, all these emotions "lumped together under the name of friendship."

While his fictional creatures might not have the rarefied aura of Robert Graves's "White Goddess" they are sovereign in their own worlds.

Ulysses

When Italy entered the war in 1915, Trieste was declared an occupied zone and if he had stayed he was danger of being interned. Moreover, all his pupils had been conscripted into the army. Stanislaus, who had spoken out against the Austro-Hungarian empire, was for his candidness sent to a camp but not the wily James—"a Jesuit for life, a Jesuit for diplomacy." So it was time to move elsewhere. With Nora and the children he returned to Zurich and there continued the seven years of labour on *Ulysses*, on which he had to duplicate as "lyricist, mathematico, astronomico, mechanico, geometrico, chemico, and arsthetic." He was also to become prone to fits, ulcers, and a large number of eye complaints. He said once that there was room in a man's heart for one novel only and that the others are always the same, artistically masked. He liked to remind himself that he had begun this vast undertaking in his mid-thirties, the same age as Dante was when he started his great *Divine Comedy* and Shakespeare wrestled with his Dark Lady of the sonnets.

Ulysses is a quintessence of everything he had seen, heard and overheard, consecration and desecration, at once serious and comical, hermetic and skittish, full of consequence and in-consequence, sounds and silences, lappings and anapests, horse hoofs and oxen thud; a motley crew of Dubliners on

16 June 1904—in acknowledgment of Joyce and Nora's first tryst.

Taken baldly the story is quite conventional, the characters neither tragic nor heroic: a host of Dubliners and in particular Stephen Dedalus, Molly Bloom and her husband Leopold Bloom; depicted in "an uninterrupted unrolling of thought"—a method which Joyce first came across in a novel by Edouard Dujardin but, as he said, he was giving Dujardin "cake for bread."

Stephen, the embryo Telemachus, leaves his lodgings in the Martello tower, walks into Dublin, takes a question-and-answer class, parries with his superior, then goes to Sandymount strand where his aesthetic reverie is jolted by needles of conscience and his idealization of young girls as innocent seabirds contrasted with pictures of whores and their she-fiends' whiteness. At nightfall, he will meet Leopold Bloom in the students' quarter of a maternity hospital where young men speak "in a strife of tongues" and a woman in labor struggles overlong to give birth to her bully boy.

Leopold Bloom, that womanly man, has begun his day by going out to buy kidneys for his breakfast. On his return he picks up the post and recognizes a letter from Molly's paramour ("His quickened heart slowed at once") Blazes Boylan, who is also her manager for singing engagements. At ten o'clock he sets out for work, a fairly dilatory task of canvassing advertisements for the *Freeman* newspaper. En route he collects an illicit letter waiting for him at a poste restante address where he is known as Henry Flower. It is from Martha Clifford, a lovelorn typist. He drops into a church hoping to hear sacred music, is disappointed; orders face lotion for his wife, visits the public baths, goes to a funeral in Glasnevin along with four pontificating Dubliners, has a glass of burgundy, goes to the National Library to check out old advertisements in the back issues of newspapers, buys a saucy book, *Sweets of Sin*, for his wife, partakes of an early supper in the dining room of the Ormond Hotel, glimpses his rival Blazes Boylan who has come in for a quick tipple, overhears Simon Dedalus, father of Stephen, sing a lament about exile and separation, is unnerved by the knowledge that Boylan will soon be privy with Mrs. Bloom, tries to blot it out, can't, addresses his dead son with a rueful exclamation—"Hate. Love. Those are names. Rudi. Soon I am old." Later he is harangued by a fervent Irish citizen, takes himself for a consoling walk on Sandymount beach where, as luck has it, his roving eye falls on Gerty MacDowell, herself filled with mutinous longings. Knowing that she will succumb, Bloom remonstrates with himself—"At it again?" His next stop is the maternity hospital where Mrs. Mina Purefoy, the one with the Methodist husband, has been accouched for three days while the medical students, those votaries of levity, distract themselves with drink and ditties.

> First he tickled her
> Then he patted her
> Then he passed the female catheter
> For he was a medical
> Jolly old medi . . .

Later in the evening, he and Stephen Dedalus (who is somewhat intoxicated) repair to Bella Cohen's brothel, a den of grotesqueness. Copulations with the living are interrupted by confrontations with the dead—an icy Shakespeare, crowned by the reflection of an antlered hat stand, and Stephen's mother, eyeless, toothless, in leper gray, a spectacle redolent of

Macbeth's witches telling that she loved him long ago when he lay in her womb and warning him to beware. "Shite," he says in retaliation and smashes a lampshade. He will not serve. Non serviam!

On the way to No. 7 Eccles Street, they repair to a cab shelter for a sobering cup of coffee and thence to the Bloom household, the long-sought Ithaca. Bloom is restored to the nuptial bed and falls asleep beside his wife Molly, the "clou" of the book named after the faithful Penelope. Molly is a marvel of licentiousness, noddle and non-guilt, as wise to her husband's dalliances as to every other miscreant walking the earth, refuses to have a maid in the house for fear of her cajoling Bloom in the WC, but wouldn't mind a young boy, imagines him seeing her garters and turning red, gloating on her by the hour. She remembers many a thing: her husband plabbery, the black closed breeches he made her buy, her labor when bringing forth her daughter Milly, the romping with Boylan earlier on, a corset she would like to get, the mountains and the meadows, the abundance of nature with fine cattle going about fields of oats, flowers of all sorts and shapes springing up out of the ditches, primroses and violets, her first kiss under the Moorish wall, Bloom's wooing of her, her torrent of images ending in a cluster of yeses.

Language is the hero and heroine, language in constant fluxion and with a dazzling virtuosity. All the given notion about story, character, plot, and human polarizings are capsized. By comparison, most other works of fiction are pusillanimous. Faulkner thought himself Joyce's spiritual heir and while the breathlessness of language in Faulkner is sometimes comparable, Joyce's characters are more graspingly human and Dublin not merely backdrop for their venality but as rich and musical as themselves. No other writer so effulgently and so ravenously recreated a city.

To each chapter he gave a title, a scene, an hour, an organ, an art, a color, a symbol and a technique; so that we are in tower, school, strand, house, bath, graveyard, newspaper office, tavern, library, street, concert room, second tavern, a strand again, a lying-in hospital, a brothel, a house and a big bed. The organs include kidney, genitals, heart, brain, ear, eye, nose, womb, nerves, flesh, and skeleton. The symbols vary from horse to tide, to nymph, to Eucharist, to virgin, to Fenian, to whore, to earth. The technic ranges from narcissism to gigantism, from tumescence to hallucination, and the styles so variable that the eighteen episodes could really be described as eighteen novels between the one cover.

Joyce had always loved Homer's hero Odysseus, not for his warring prowess but for his cunning. The arsenal was for lesser men. *Ulysses* he placed higher than Hamlet, Don Quixote or Faust. It was the human traits in Odysseus that he admired: a man who did not court bloodshed and who saw war as an outlet for the marketeers. When the recruiting officer found him plowing, his little son alongside him, Odysseus feigned madness so as not to be enlisted. Suspecting a trick, they laid the little boy into a furrow and naturally Odysseus had to hold the plow back. Once recruited into the Greek army, he was among the soldiers secreted in the wooden horse which defeated Troy. His long route back to Ithaca made him, for Joyce, a far greater hero than Achilles or Agamemnon. The Greek hero was to have a modern equivalent in the person of Leopold Bloom whose conquests were decidedly unbloody.

It would be years before he commenced on it. He would have been crushed by the reception for his play *Exiles* in

Munich, which was described as an "Irish stew," and he would be battling to find a publisher for *A Portrait of the Artist* and constantly moving "the caravan of his family" from one small apartment to another.

He rarely spoke of the war and he never wrote about it. He believed that politics and government were for specialists and he was a specialist in only one thing. The 1916 rebellion in Dublin he deemed useless. Yeats, on the other hand, wrote magnificently of the small posse of dedicated men who had raised the Irish flag above the Post Office and were soon to be executed. Years later Joyce told the Polish novelist Jan Parandowski that there was fighting on all fronts, that empires fell, kings went into exile, the old order was collapsing but he worked with the conviction that he was doing something for the most distant future. He may not have gone to the battlefront but he was in the trenches with himself every day, weaving and unweaving; staccato sounds, broken chords and so uncanny a re-creation of Dublin that he reckoned it would serve as a blueprint if the city were ever to be destroyed.

Ulysses did not appear in the United States until twenty years after its inception, the repeal coinciding with the repeal against Prohibition, prompting one of Joyce's allies to remark that minds and bottles had been opened at the same time. Judge Woolsey, the United States District Court judge, determined at the trial that the book was not "dirt for dirt's sake." He did not "detect the leer of the sensualist," and therefore wished to prove that the book was not pornographic, something which the New York Society for the Prevention of Vice had built their case on. Judge Woolsey did a great thing for Joyce and for literature but reading his pronouncement it is clear that the vertiginous influence of the master had got the better of him.

He spoke of the "screen of consciousness with its ever-shifting kaleidoscopic impressions" carrying, "as it were on a plastic palimpsest, not only what is in the focus of each man's observation of the actual things about him, but also in a penumbral zone residua of past impressions, some recent and some drawn up by association from the domain of the subconscious."

Anyone who touched Joyce seemed to get a bit carried away and makes us cry out as Molly Bloom did: "O, rocks! Tell us in plain words." Stuart Gilbert mentions "divine afflatus [which] begins to swell the creative cyst" and "the wallet of winds [like that which] Aeolus gave to Odysseus," while some other scribe talks of "the misty nebula of erotic light taking on a purely coprologic significance." Another pundit dilating on the existential significance of the chamber pot in Molly's bedroom, decided that it was a symbol for our era of waste and that the orange beading on the handle was in deference to the flag of Gibraltar. O rocks. Joyce chose his words "in the baldest and coldest way" and he used them like a marksman. He said he had all the words, it was simply a question of putting them in the right order. He would pore over each word not only for its rhythm, its sense, its aptness, its beauty, its vulgarity, its myriad associativeness, but sometimes for its prophetic core. Every word, like every image, was up for investigation. Even then he was dissatisfied. He wanted a language above all languages, he refused to be enclosed in any tradition. He wanted to be God.

Shamelessly he marshaled friends and acquaintances to supply him with anecdotes, or even talk to him about Leopold Bloom. His correspondence from Trieste with his friend Frank Budgen in Zurich gives us some idea of the scrupulousness of his research along with his scalding wit. A catchword was enough to set him off. He pointed out to Budgen the good use he made of any bit of blarney told to him. From friends in Dublin, he would need to know the type of pianola in Bella Cohen's brothel, the lamp which Stephen Dedalus would smash with his ashplant when the ghost of his dead mother appears, and the pretty music-hall airs that might be played. "My Girl's a Yorkshire Girl" was what he decided on. And Homer, always returning to Home. Hermes had given Ulysses a moly flower to protect him from Circe's wiles. This moly flower was "a hard nut to crack." It was a white flower with a black root and was said to have magic propensities. It led to a train of questions. Would it be an invisible influence against accident? What accident might that be? Syphilis, he thought, then wondered if the etymology of syphilis was swine love or syn phileis, the conjoining of humans. And could moly also be absinthe which made men impotent, the juice of chastity, the forestalling unction? He had corresponded with the Baroness St. Leger, "a siren of the Lago Maggiore," who had assured him that the moly was the garlic flower. He chose Hermes because he was the god of signposts, shepherd to Leopold Bloom. Greece and Dublin, the ancient and the modern, lumped into one.

There he was, working ten hours a day, equipped with rhyming dictionaries, maps, street directories, Gilbert's *History of Dublin*, badgering his friends for precise information on this or that, list of shops, the steps up to 7 Eccles Street; asking his faithful Aunt Josephine to get a page of foolscap and scribble down any goddamn drivel that came into her head, to find out about the freezing winter of 1893 and if the canals were frozen hard enough for people to skate on. After each episode he would collapse and repair to a bedroom, his eyesight worse than ever, his wife having to nurse him, and listen to the expletives, "Damn Homer, damn Ulysses, and damn Bloom."

But his powers of recuperation were great and soon he would be up again, teaching, writing, visiting the tavern and the brothels, "the most interesting places in any city." Stanislaus who had moved to another apartment would be sent a note asking how they were supposed to eat, while Joyce often deferred eviction by playing a tune to his hire-purchase piano and bamboozled a landlord to give them a week or a month's extension. The trials of home life did not seem to hit him, at least not yet. Zurich was full of stimulation. Greeks, Poles, Germans, conscientious objectors, artists, chancers, and spies, had all convened in the same city and frequented the Pfauen Café where he himself drank and overheard crackpot theories of futurism, cubism and Dadaism.

His listeners must have been enthralled by this lank, sandy-haired Irishman, with the near boneless handshake and the supple wit, questioning each on what he knew best. He copied their slang and their anecdotes onto slips of paper which he consigned to his pockets. He spoke five languages and had as well a smattering of Greek, though not classical Greek. Greeks meant good luck, nuns ill luck. He would have to know if the pigeons which flew between Scylla and Charybdis bore a resemblance to the Dublin ones and he welcomed anatomical descriptions of the sirens in their coral caves, poised to bewitch the sailors. Each country and therefore each countryman had his own bit of private lore and mob manners to impart. He questioned the locals on the spring rite in which the winter demon dressed in cotton was placed on a wooden pyre and set fire to. He copied down French songs and he particularly liked the scatological ones. He carried a pair of miniature doll's drawers which he would put two fingers into and dangle puppet-like on the counter table to the amusement of the motley clientele. In a more ponderous mood, he lectured Frank Budgen on the importance of that august garment.

Austin Clarke, a Dublin poet, said many years later that when they met in Paris, Joyce was eager to hear the latest smutty stories circulating among Dublin schoolboys. Clarke thought Joyce was afflicted "with a particular kind of Irish pornography," but that he was also a dreamer. Dreamer and dredger, gerund purveyor and ultimate wordsmith, he would lope his way home, dancing capriciously in his cups, reciting Verlaine, and yet be ready for the next day's excruciating work, to embody the jokes, the smut, the ditties, the flotsam and jetsam of all that he had heard so as to make his book more universal and commodious. For a lesser writer these dissipations would have been ruinous but he had to experience everything in order to write it. It was not simply that. He would astound his readers. He would bring them to a pitch of consciousness where they had not gone before. Not for him the "experimentation" of Marcel Proust, of whom he said: "Analytic still life. Reader knows end of sentence before him." He would breach unknown frontiers.

"[A]pproach an ink-bottle," he wrote to Frank Budgen. Budgen had been a sailor and for Joyce his experiences at sea, sea stories, sea slang, the sexual pangs of the sailors, had to be transferred into the mouths of the aroused Dublin wanderers. After months of begging and cajoling Budgen obliged by coming in person to Paris. The revels got headier. They stayed out late, still later, Joyce insisting when the bar closed that they be admitted to an upstairs parlor and in the small hours when they did make their way home, Joyce in his straw hat and cane performed his Isadora Duncan impersonation, a matter of whirling arms, high-kicking legs, and grimaces which Budgen likened to the ritual antics of a comic religion. They laughed a lot, wakened the neighbors and returned to an irate Nora Barnacle shouting out the window and demanding that these revels stop. They didn't. They couldn't. Nothing could dampen Joyce's abundance of spirit and laughter during those his richest and most exhaustive years. In one of these night fracases, Nora told him that she had torn up his manuscript and it sobered him enough to ransack the apartment and find it. The book "ist ein Schwein," she said. Carousing was only part of the saga; there was another side to him that very few saw, hurrying from one tuition job to the next, or one creditor to the next, not laughing, not smiling but as the novelist Italo Svevo noted, "locked in the inner isolation of his being."

Between him and Nora there was friction. Writers are a scourge to those they cohabit with. They are present and at the same time they are absent. They are present by the fact of their continuing curiosity, their needs, their cataloguing minds, their longing to see into another person, a longing that is increasingly discharged into the work. The bulk of his time when he was not teaching he was in one of the bedrooms, a suitcase lid on his lap as a desk, bringing to life streets, shops, awnings, sayings, the "Druid silence" of the sea and sweethearts on the swings in Stephen's Green, their shadows coupling. The photographs of Nora with her growing children show us a less jaunty, a far more solemn woman with an unreadiness to smile. She was homesick without wanting to go home. To a maid she would talk on about Ireland and how quick the clothes dried on the line but, as Joyce said, she detested her race. She was becoming wife and mother and less and less "the blue mountain flower." From time to time in his letters, he would refer to her nerves or her nervous breakdown or her fears as her hair began to fall out. Marriage in its wintry discontent.

But all was not gloom. He was gathering admirers, little windfalls of money as chapters of *A Portrait of the Artist* appeared in literary magazines in England and America. Ezra Pound placed him above all living writers and took upon himself the stalwart task of getting *A Portrait* published in England. When Pound read what Edward Garnett had written for Duckworth, the publishers, he fumed, suggesting first and foremost that Garnett be sent to the Serbian front to take him out of harm's way, then added that he would not pass on these pulings to an imbecile, let alone James Joyce himself. Garnett had described the book as "too discursive, formless, unrestrained, and ugly things, ugly words are too prominent . . ." Pound said that the remarks were typical of the venom and the envy which befouls literature and as for asking James Joyce for cuts—which the publishers had suggested—it would be tantamount to fitting "the Venus de Milo into a piss-pot."

Pound and Yeats tried to secure a grant for him from the Royal Literary Fund, but met with no success. Miss Harriet Weaver, editor of the *Little Review*, was so touched by "the piercing spirit" of his work that she resolved to give him a trimonthly allowance of fifty pounds from her capital while the war lasted. The next bounty was from a more worldly source, Mrs. Harold (Edith Rockefeller) McCormick, a devotee of Karl Gustav Jung and a patron of the arts in Zurich. She was bestowing a fellowship of 12,000 francs, with 1,000 to be paid each month. He had to borrow a black suit in order to present himself to the bank manager and that night in the café it was double liters of Nostrano wine.

But gifts come with a price and his did, with the exception of Miss Weaver's. Mrs. McCormick cursorily stopped her allowance and refused to meet with Joyce in answer to one of his craven letters. As always, he believed a friend had betrayed him. This friend Ottocaro Weiss, he insisted, had probably told the good lady of his aversion for Jung and Jung in turn had advised her to stop doling out money, that a spartan existence might help to pull him back from dissolution. It did not occur to him that Mrs. McCormick was as capricious as many another tycoon. From his literary well-wishers in England, he heard that in return for the hundred pounds from the privy purse, it would be appreciated if he would do something for the Allied cause, in short, if he could write some journalism. He couldn't, so instead he launched into another enterprise that would not only take him from his work but would land him in "phthisis." With his friend the actor Claud Sykes, he decided to assemble a group, named The English Players, who would perform in Swiss towns. He chose Irish plays—among them Synge's *Riders to the Sea* (which Nora acted in) and Oscar Wilde's *The Importance of Being Earnest*—and took on the several roles of dramaturge, coacher, prompter, and, most reckless of all, business manager.

It was not long before there was an altercation with his puerile English colleagues. Joyce may have disliked the strangling mentality of Catholic Ireland but it was matched by an equal distaste for English imperialism. Henry Carr, a British ex-soldier, who now worked in the British Consulate, was cast in a minor part of Wilde's play and had treated himself to a pair of trousers. Joyce, as bursar, paid Carr half what he had paid the leading actors and demanded a reimbursement for five tickets which Carr had got for his friends. Carr rounded on him and said that he had not only been insulted by the pittance he was paid, but he expected reimbursement for the trousers. Things got heated, Carr accusing Joyce of being "a cad and a swindler," a man too cowardly to enlist for military service. Joyce was outraged. Carr threatened to have him removed from the Consulate by force. Nothing for it but litigation. His bile against the English took on a fresh momentum and led to amelioration towards the Irish. "An Irish safety pin," he insisted, was "worth more than an English epic." He praised the German offensive, changed his daily newspaper to a pro-German one, dismissed these king's representatives as no-nos, functionaries whose bills were paid by men like his father to look after Joyce's interests abroad. Lloyd George, the Prime Minister, to whom he had appealed, wished the English players success but nothing more. It was from that to the courts at Lausanne; Joyce suing Carr for the price of five unpaid tickets, Carr counterclaiming for the trousers, and Joyce seeking substantive rewards for the threat of assault and libel in a municipal office. It ended several months later with Carr losing on one point, Joyce losing on another but having to part with half the contents of his wallet when the bailiff called at his apartment to collect his fine, even threatening to take his books and his typewriter. Joyce's valediction was put to rhyme:

Up to rheumy Zurich came an Irishman one day
As the town was rather dull he thought he'd give a play,
So that German propagandists might be rightly riled
But the bully British philistine once more made Oscar wild.

So it was back to the cramped bedroom, the various-colored inks, and the suitcase lid, the contrasting potions of incense, Mariolatry, masturbation and stewed cockles along with a deterioration of his eyesight which he believed Circe had caused because of the unpleasant things he had ascribed to her legend.

Ulysses was written in three cities: first Trieste, which he returned to after the war, then Zurich, and then Paris which he visited at Ezra Pound's suggestion and where he remained for twenty years. There were times during the seven-year labor of *Ulysses* when its author too was "on the rocks." Fragments that he had written were in this place and that and one letter to Italo Svevo demonstrates Joyce's confounding mixture of chaos and exigence. There was, he told Svevo, in his brother-in-law's apartment on the fourth floor an oilcloth briefcase fastened with a rubber band which had the color of a nun's belly approximately ninety-five by seventy centimeters which he was in urgent need of to finish "the bitch-of-mother book." In it were the "written symbols of the languid lights" which had flashed across his soul. There were other things less easy for a public to stomach. His technical monstrosities, his anti-humanist indifference, his desecration of style and his obsession with bodily functions which bordered on the macabre. He would be accused of all that and more and he countered by saying that obscenity occurs in the pages of life as well. More importantly he would say that "the measure of a work of art is from how deep a life does it spring." His is immeasurable.

Sirens

THE PROGRESS OF *Ulysses* was for its author the progress of a sandblast, his audacity increasing with every chapter as he found different organs, colors, techniques and styles, so much so that T. S. Eliot was to say that Joyce had exposed the futility of all style. There were danger signals. Even Miss Weaver was unnerved and began to see "a weakening or diffusion of some sort." She blamed it on his financial worries. Ezra Pound asked him to explain the method (or methods) of his madness.

Smarting under these rebukes he felt that he must come to his own defense. He was doing something completely new and his method was in no way capricious. Writing to Miss Weaver, on whom he depended for emotional and financial sustenance, he emphasized that each section by nature of its wandering theme required different music, different cadences, different styles, and to shirk that would be a disservice. An understanding of the work would come only when all the elements were fused together. He admitted that there may be some who would wish that he did not experiment so, just as there were those who thought Odysseus should never have left his native land, should have stayed bound to the rock of Ithaca, but where was the adventure in that? As an afterthought he could not resist the boast that George Lidwell, the solicitor who had defected in the row

over *Dubliners*, and who had found his way into *Ulysses* as a
useless swain, had suddenly died. Lidwell appeared in the
Sirens section, one of the most audacious pieces of literature
ever written. His "fugue" as he calls it begins with the vice-
regal carriage driving out of Phoenix Park, then centers on
the early lunch hubbub in the bar of the Ormond Hotel—
hoofirons, steelyringing, Idolores . . . Jingle jingle jaunted jin-
gling . . . Coins. Clocks . . . Clapclop. Clipclap. Clappyclap.

It is hard to imagine the shock for those reading it for the
first time. To his two ardent American editors Miss Heap and
Miss Anderson who serialized it in the *Little Review*, it boded
trouble. Margaret Anderson admitted to having cried upon
reading the opening lines of the *Proteus* section in which
Stephen Dedalus, walking on Sandymount beach, declares,
"Signatures of all things I am here to read, seaspawn and sea-
wrack, the nearing tide." She had not read anything so beautiful or so transcending in her whole life and promised to print
episodes of *Ulysses* if it was the last thing she did. Chapters ran
intermittently over a period of three years but trouble struck
when the "marmaladey" section was confiscated by order of the
United States Post Office and the magazine burnt.

To us now Episode 10 is a dazzling feat of sound and narrative, a tableau in which the high and the low, the nobs and the
lame pass along the city of Dublin, their encounters punctuated
with broken chords of sound and sharp sarcastic interjection.
The horse and carriage bringing the lord lieutenant, the Earl of
Dudley, and his entourage in pearl gray and eau de Nil, passes
through the lower gates of Phoenix Park, drives up the northern
quays over Bloody Bridge, the party saluted by some but not by
others, not for instance by a pedestrian who while itching his

nose debates whether he would arrive more quickly at Phibs-borough by a triple change of tram, by hailing a car, or going on foot.

Gerty MacDowell, whom we are later to meet in swooning capitulation, cranes her neck to see what her excellency has on. A second woman gets only a glimpse of a sunshade and wheel spokes in the sun's glare. The sun is shining. Blazes Boylan in tan shoes and straw hat, with a red flower between his lips, gives the ladies in the carriage the benefit of his ardent gaze—"by my wild gaze I thee gander." He will be privy with Mrs. Bloom at four but first he has a sortie into the Ormond bar to greet the barmaids—the Sirens—and enjoy a syrupy sloe gin. Inside the counter bronze-haired Miss Douce and gold-haired Miss Kennedy officiate. Pinnacles of hair. Black satin blouse that's made of stuff that cost two-and-nine a yard.

"Aren't men frightful idiots?" from Miss Douce to Miss Kennedy.

Mr. Bloom soon enters the inner room where bald Pat, a waiter of sorts, takes his order. Mashed potatoes and liver if you please. While preparing to pen a clandestine love letter Mr. Bloom muses on life's sad fare, time passing and so on. Can't bring it back. Like trying to hold water in a muslin. Miss Bronze undoes buttons of black blouse to see if she has got a sunburn from recent vacation in Rostrevor in County Down. She hasn't. A bit of borax with cherry laurel water will do it, according to the wisdom of Miss Gold. Mr. Dedalus senior, father of the demurring Stephen, presses Miss Douce's hand, visualiz-ing hair shreds, maiden hair, mermaidness. "Thanks awfully muchly." Mr. Lenehan proposes a riddle. The stork and the fox riddle. The men quaff the nectar bowl. There are no lady

customers. Boylan lifts the lid of the piano and peddles a muf-
fled hammerfall.

In the dining room Mr. Bloom, aware of his rival in the outer
precincts, takes out two sheets of cream vellum to write his
lovelorns. Miss Kennedy lifts and relifts her skirt, allows elas-
tic garter to rebound against her warm, smackable, nicely
hosed thigh and scolds the men for making free with her. Her
lips all but humming, the rose on her breast rising falling.
Clock clacks. Stillness and sound. First one then the other. A
limbo. The cool dim green of ocean-green shadow. Sunlight
screened by a gold cross-blind. Nothing and everything hap-
pening at once. A sifting of various thoughts, a ringing cash
register, a "by Japers," an unfinished sentence—"why did he
go so quick when I?" Random communion and banter between
the drinkers but also a disquieting separateness. Mr. Dedalus
and bald Pat having a private conflab as to whether Bloom
knows where buccaneer Boylan is heading for. And to a lady no
better than him—"a backside on her like a ball alley." Bloom
does know, feels the pain—"I, he, old, young." He defers the
thinking of it and allows the passing images to buoy him along.
Jealousy is for smaller men, men with sanitary minds. Clean
table, fresh flowers, napkins like miters, good value—"Best
value in Dublin."

Simon Dedalus stands tall and brave, stretches out his
hand, commences a song about exile, a sail upon the billows.
Soon a girl's veil and two tiny flutters. Balm against the outside
world. Later there will be arguments, a hurling of a biscuit tin,
evening fireworks, mutual ejaculation, a stalled birth, drunken-
ness, remorse and Mrs. Bloom's phantasmagoric ruminations
about the et ceteras of jimjam lick itup fleshy love.

In the bar, bars of music, another voice, loud, full, shiny, avenging the treachery wreaked on the Croppy Boy, foully duped by the Conqueror. Politics, history, sentimentality and loss. Mr. Bloom swayed by the musical ambience pens his letter, refers to the sad in life while also hoping that she will enjoy the "pres: p. o. two-and-six." Such musings lead him to think of his dead son and wrings from him a most baleful cry—"Hate. Love. Those are names, Rudy. Soon I am old."

And soon and begob the dinner bustle will cease, the doors be closed for the lull hour, men sleeping off their torpor, Boylan arriving at No. 7 Eccles Street and admitted to Molly's sanctum. Bloom never one for the confrontation sets out on his goat wander, passes a blind stripling, the tap tap tap stick, then a frowsy whore, her hat askew, she whom he once knew in her prime. Lonely he feels.

His author no doubt was aware of impending storm. The commotion with his fugue was a matter of stylistic prodigality but the subsequent chapter named *Nausikaa* was an insult to the mores and morals of America. As he heard that issues of the *Little Review* were being burned, Joyce the joker said that by being burned twice on earth he would possibly be ensured a quick passage through purgatory. Mr. John S. Sumner, Secretary of the New York Society for the Suppression of Vice, lodged a formal complaint and Miss Anderson was summoned to a court in Greenwich Village before three judges and some intrigued New Yorkers. John Quinn, who had befriended Joyce, acted as defending solicitor but his irritation with the lady editors was such that he secretly wished their magazine would be sent back to the stockyards in Chicago and pulped. Joyce seemed not to have that much concern for his stalwarts and even voiced the hope that the case would be as notorious as that of *Madame Bovary* sixty years before. He always guessed that the Nausikaa episode would bring trouble. When writing it he described it to Frank Budgen as a "namby-pamby jammy marmalady drawersy (alto là!) style with effects of incense, mariolatry, masturbation, stewed cockles, painter's palette, chitchat, circumlocutions, etc. etc."

To help him with his researches and understand the mushiness of Gerty MacDowell, the errant one, he wrote to his pious Aunt Josephine for novelettes and penny hymnbooks. Little did she know what she was abetting. As with every chapter, *Nausikaa* has an organ, an art, a symbol and a technic. The symbol was the Virgin, the setting close to the Star of the Sea Church and a retreat in progress. The technic is tumescence and detumescence, the swelling and limpness of the male genital.

It is the most seductive chapter in *Ulysses*. Gerty and her two girlfriends, Edy and Cissy, have gone to the sea, to relax and discuss matters feminine. Cissy has squalling twins, and Edy has a baby dribbling in a go-cart—all anathema to Gerty's romantic longings. The words of the litany from the Star of the Sea Church—"Tower of ivory, tower of gold," those paeans to the Virgin Mary intrude on Gerty's erotic stirrings as her "womanflower" raises the specter of a "manflower" in a gentleman not too far away. Our Leopoldo has appeared, eyeing her "as a snake eyes its prey" and very soon she realizes that she has "raised the devil in him." The distractions are irking, what with the litany, the noisy children, and a ball being passed back and forth, when all Gerty wanted was a bit of sea air to drive away her blues! Not that that was all Gerty wanted. Gerty has luxurious notions for herself. She is the sort of girl who takes care of her looks, swallows jelloids to give her strength, and applies lemon juice and a queen of ointments to whiten her hands. She has cut her hair that morning on account of the new moon and is within her limited means a thorough slave to "Dame Fashion." She is wearing an electric blue blouse, home tinted with dolly dyes, has a wad of cottonwool soaked in her favorite perfume and undies slotted with ribbon which she has washed and blued. She also has a gnawing hunger for that thing called "pure love." The attentions of the gentleman make her wax poetic and soon she imagines herself eating violets or roses as well as picturing herself as a wife with wifely skills, lighting fires and making griddlecakes.

She who crimsons at rude words, this veritable model of young Catholic girlhood, soon yields to the glances of the mysterious stranger. When the children kick the ball along the weedy rocks, he is sporting enough to kick it back but aims in the direction of Gerty's slender calves. Under the brim of her chocolate straw hat, she sees a face worn but passionate, and as the incense drifts out from the open window of the church, the pronouncements of the mystical rose become a little less mystical with each devouring glance. Because of his wearing black, Gerty concludes that the man is in deep mourning and thinks maybe he has had a wife who has just died or gone to the madhouse. Cissy, anxious to strike up a friendship with the strange man, runs on her gandery legs to ask him the time. His watch has stopped. His watch has stopped because this is the author's way of reminding us that Leopold Bloom is trying to defer the remembrance of the moment when his wife's paramour is being admitted to his house at No. 7 Eccles Street, and instead engages with the ladylike Gerty.

How near or how far Bloom and Gerty are from each other, we never know. It is all in the mind and in the words. Consummation is reached through a series of devices, Gertie swinging her legs in and out and feeling the warmth of her flesh against her stays as she gazes at the fireworks from a nearby bazaar. As Roman candles burst up into the sky Gerty leans far back, her face suffused with a divine blush to give the gentleman a view of her nainsook knickers, the secret lovers reach zeniths. Trembling in every limb, Gerty would feign have cried chokingly to him to welcome him into her snowy-white arms but she daren't. For him it is not quite so ethereal—"Up like a rocket, down like a stick."

Soon Bloom, "the spent brute," mutely asks forgiveness, signals Gerty that she not tell it, a thousand times not tell it. It would be their secret. As she walks away, he notices that she has a limp and feels mildly sorry for her. He wonders if her excitement was intensified because of being close to her monthlies and then tries to estimate how many women in the city of Dublin on that very evening would have monthlies. His thoughts run on to the number of virgins in the city all going mad and to the nuns cooped up in various convents, berserk for that which they cannot get and baring their teeth at one another. He smoothes out his wet shirt, feels his skin cold and clammy and ponders what they might have said had they spoken. Better that they hadn't. He is reminded of a prostitute in Meath Street and of the words he made her mouth say in the dark. He is both exhilarated and let down. As he walks away he wonders if she will come back tomorrow, if they both will, the way criminals do. Going along he vexes the thick sand with a stick and writes a message for her, but knows that some tramp will flatten it out with his feet by morning. Transitory passion washed away. He flings the stick, his wooden pen, into "silted sand."

In the court in Greenwich Village John Quinn had brought three doyens of culture, an editor, a member of the Theatre

Guild and the writer John Cowper Powys to testify to the beauty of the work and the assurance that it could not corrupt young girls. Mr. Moeller, the member of the guild, unwisely tried to compare its importance to the innovative works of Sigmund Freud. When the moment came for the offending passages which Mr. Sumner had selected to be read out, one of the judges asked that Miss Anderson be removed from the court as an act of propriety. He seemed to have forgotten that she had published the material or else assumed that, like the Serbian printer she had employed, it was "double Dutch" to her. The other two judges found it so incomprehensible that they asked for a week's respite to collect their faculties and read the entire episode. When the trial resumed things got fractious. John Quinn contended that Gerty's exhibition of her drawers was not nearly so flagrant as the skimpy attire of mannequins in Fifth Avenue. The prosecuting attorney became so apoplectic that Quinn pounced on him and cited it as clear evidence that *Ulysses* did not corrupt or fill people with sexual urges, but in fact did the opposite, it made them implode with anger. The judges laughed at this ruse but nevertheless the editors were convicted, fined fifty pounds each and forbidden to publish any more installments of *Ulysses*.

For Joyce it was a repetition of the slaughter of *Dubliners*. Various publishers in New York who had expressed some interest in the book were no longer prepared to publish it because of a fear of prosecution and he said despairingly, "My book will never come out now."

Miss Beach

Yet for his art he always found what he wanted. Waiting in the wings was Sylvia Beach, a bright birdlike young woman who had come from Baltimore and made a niche for herself in bohemian Paris with her bookshop Shakespeare & Company. Her shop was salon, post office, lending library and impromptu bank for a clutch of American writers but it was Joyce whom she coveted for her literary galaxy.

The story has been told again and again, the fairy-tale encounter as she came upon him at a party in his tennis shoes and old jacket, standing somewhat aloof. She approached him and said, "Is this the great James Joyce?" "James Joyce," he replied. When she handed him her card he had to cross to the window, on account of his poor eyesight, to read it. In keeping with his ever-superstitious nature he was pleased to find the word "Shakespeare" and took it to be a good omen. A year later he called on her to hear a proposal which she had been nurturing. Would she pay him the honor of allowing her to publish *Ulysses*? Joyce was incredulous. For all his burgeoning fame, he was living in an old flat with no electricity, no bathtub and a few cracked plates and here was a woman assuring him that she could find enough subscribers, and important ones at that, to bring *Ulysses* to the world. The printer she had already decided on, an intellectual in Dijon called Maurice Darantiere whom she knew through her companion Adrienne Monnier who also owned a bookshop. She proposed that they print 1,000 copies, 100 signed on Holland paper, 150 on de luxe paper and the remaining 750 on linen. She would give the author 66 percent of the net profits.

Neither Miss Beach nor M. Darantiere could have guessed the complications which lay ahead because neither of them knew James Joyce. In his possession there was only a carbon copy of *Ulysses* which did not carry the changes he had made from the various published versions in serial form. As he set about embodying these changes from memory he added so much that the book expanded by one-third during that dizzying period. Moreover his corrections were almost illegible, written in his cramped, weblike handwriting. His demands about paper, binding and typeface were inflexible. Typists were somehow procured—and lost—in this fever of work and revision. Joyce was in a state of "energetic prostration" but so were some of his helpmates. Some were so shocked by the material that they dismissed themselves. A Mrs. Harrison ran into trouble with her English husband who was so scandalized by what he read that he threw the pages into the fire. Another Veronica to Joyce's Jesus, this brave crusader rescued them but some particles were lost and the missing lines had to be retrieved from John Quinn in New York. Wherever Joyce went there was chaos. He was still writing to friends to borrow "bits" of them for his Jarvey or his sailor impersonations as well as finishing the last chapter which he called "his most secret conception."

He insisted on five sets of proofs, was constantly making changes, the corrected pages so scarred with stars and lineations that the beleaguered printer threatened to withdraw, as these cosmic, physical, psychical congeries were driving him askew! Throughout it all Miss Beach remained sanguine. The Greek flag fluttered outside her shop alerting passersby to the great and pending event. It was of course her halcyon time, the most famous, albeit unread book in the world being published by her and about to be exhibited in her shop. A conference cum séance was held in Miss Monnier's bookstore, La Maison des Amis des Livres, at 7, rue de l'Odéon, and the French critic Valery Larbaud spoke of Joyce's revolutionary technique—his "stream of consciousness."

Joyce wanted the cobalt blue of the Greek flag on his cover but finding the correct paper to reproduce that exact blue meant M. Darantiere had to journey to Germany and Holland, then submit samples to the author who did not feel that the white lettering on blue had the magic impact of white islands on a blue archipelago of water.

Meanwhile, Miss Beach was gathering subscribers. They included Hemingway, Winston Churchill, André Gide, an Anglican bishop, several French intellectuals but not George Bernard Shaw. Shaw declined, adding that it was a repulsive and accurate description of Ireland and that he would like to force every Irish male to read it but that the cost was exorbitant. He then indulged in a bit of chiding, saying that no doubt as a young beglamoured barbarian the book seemed to her to be art, but was in fact a slice of Dublin life.

Joyce worked day and night but at the same time refused to be harried by his printer who was rapidly beginning to feel the lunacy of the Irishman entering the patrician sanctum of his own household. While writing the last episode, the *Penelope* section, as the earlier sections were supposedly and agonizedly being printed, his Aunt Josephine was called on for human aspects of bygone Dublin, sundry geographic details and any juicy recollections about a certain major whom he was casting as Molly Bloom's father.

In keeping with his superstitions he wanted it published on his fortieth birthday and Darantiere managed to give two copies to the conductor of the Dijon–Paris Express. Miss Beach met the train at seven in the morning and went directly to Joyce's apartment to deliver her progeny. Joyce put a copy aside for himself, and Nora, in her roguish way, proceeded to sell it to Arthur Power, a Dubliner who was visiting. The second copy was displayed in a glass case in Miss Beach's shop and people came to look at it as they might at some religious relic. That night in an Italian restaurant Joyce had the book and after much coaxing was persuaded to undo the parcel to show it to his guests. Two waiters who did not know what it was declared it "a poem" and solemnly carried it across to the padrone for his blessing.

Ulysses was born, the placentation far lengthier and bloodier than the tortured birth of Mina Purefoy's "bully baby" in the *Oxen of the Sun* episode.

Fame

It was to Miss Beach's shop every day to learn of new subscribers, to fondle the list, to wrap up the books for the post and to propose wild and unrealistic plans for advertising it. He was alive to omens and slurs. If he saw a rat on the way he fainted. The shop as Miss Beach later said was completely at the service of James Joyce and his *Ulysses*. Arthur Power said that Sylvia Beach would have crucified herself for Joyce so long as it was done in public. To Miss Weaver in England the requests were numerous. Copies were to be sent to a host of reviewers, to influential people, to a library in Edinburgh, to the Bodleian Library in Oxford and to the British Museum. As the book was slow to receive reviews he sensed a boycott. It met with predictable volleys of praise and vituperation.

To Middleton Murry who praised it as the outpourings of a half-demented man of genius, Joyce wrote a cordial letter and another to Arnold Bennett who thought the *Penelope* section a masterpiece. He suggested to Miss Weaver that she give a nudge to T. S. Eliot to review it in the *Times Literary Supplement*. All the graceless musterings which a writer resorts to once the labor has been done. In retrospect it is something of a diminishment but it is only human. When he learned that Shane Leslie had said "that *Ulysses* had yet to take its full place in the thought and history of mankind" he asked her to have that quote circulated.

The reaction from his immediate family hurt him deeply. He may have in passing called it "a tiresome book" and even admitted that the money spent on a pound of chops would be just as wisely spent, but he raged at the slightest rejection. His Aunt Josephine, so often called upon to send him data about this or that, felt the same distaste as the Samsa family felt in Kafka's *Metamorphosis* upon finding that their son Gregor had turned into a loathsome insect. She put it in a press, then thinking its presence sacrilegious she loaned it to somebody. She was rebuked in grandiloquent tones. Did she not realize that it would be worth a hundred guineas in a given number of years? When her daughter, Kathleen, met Joyce long after and told him that her mother thought the book not fit to read, he said ruefully that if *Ulysses* was not fit to read, life was not fit to live. His father looked at passages through his monocle and said that his son was "a nice sort of blackguard." But the unkindest cut came from Nora. She read twenty-seven pages and that, as Joyce pointedly said, included the title page. He gave her a new edition with an errata sheet, which had fewer printer's errors, but it was no incentive. From what we know, Nora only read novelettes bought at railway-station kiosks and some passages of Sacher-Masoch which Joyce had given her in their sexually hoopsar days. When, years later, she went to Galway with her children in yet another and more determined effort to leave Joyce, he wrote one of his tender and self-lacerating letters calling her his dear queen and begging her even then to read "the terrible book which had broken the heart in his breast." It probably had. It broke other hearts as well. An American, Dr. Joseph Collins, who had met Joyce through a mutual friend, said that his files had writings by the insane which were just as good and then proceeded to give a medical explanation of the deterioration of Joyce's brain.

Stanislaus's praise was tepid; hardly surprising from a brother who resented such arbitrary genius. His little cavils were unfortunate. The book "lacked warmth and serenity." It was like asking a tornado to serve as a bedwarmer. As for the "stream of consciousness" Stanislaus staked his claim—"My fixed idea by the bye old chap." The *Penelope* episode repelled him, as it did many another. Rebecca West wrote of Joyce's "camouflaged sentimentality" and Virginia Woolf called it "underbred," the effort of "a queasy undergraduate scratching his pimples." T. S. Eliot while admiring it was also threatened by its audacity and wished for his own sake that he had not read it. How could anyone surpass the achievement? In the *Oxen of the Sun* episode the fecundity of coition was matched by a multiplicity of styles, those of Milton, Sir Thomas Browne, Richard Burton, Bunyan, Steele, Addison, Landor, Pater and Cardinal Newman, then deteriorating into a jumble of pidgin English, nigger English, Cockney, Irish and Bowery slang. In private Eliot said that the book gave no insight into human nature, was a dazzlement of style and not a sea of consciousness. His fellow author George Moore called it a work from the "Dublin docks"; its author a Zola gone to seed. Yeats recognized its genius and wrote to Joyce to assure him of his many admirers in Dublin.

In his half-embattled but decidedly triumphant outpost Joyce said it did not matter if his technique was "veracious" or not, it had served him as a bridge to march his eighteen episodes across, his troops were over and his opponents could blow the bridge sky-high for all he cared.

His fame spread even among those who had not read him.

His photograph on the cover of *Time* magazine alerted his family in Ireland who were both smarting from the shame of his book and wondering when they would be reimbursed. He was making new friends and losing old ones.

Fame, as Rilke has said, is the quintessence of all the mistakes which gather around a name. Legends began to spring up. He was a misanthrope, a cocaine addict, *"cavalier servante"* of duchesses, a Bolshevik propagandist, a spy for Austria during the war, the text of *Ulysses* being merely a code for British intelligence: moreover he swam in the Seine each morning, surrounded himself with mirrors, wore black gloves in bed and so on. And so on. Nothing about the twenty thousand hours of labor, his arthritis, suffusions in his eyes and in his brain, having to use charcoal sticks and different inks to see what he had written. He used to test his failing sight by trying to count the number of lights on the Place de la Concorde when he went out of an evening. True to that peculiar wonderment which never quite left him, he blamed his eye ailments upon a night's drinking at Pirano many years before when he had fallen in the gutter and believed that he got arthritis.

With the publication of *Ulysses* there came as well the distractions, the unsettledness; lobbying, cajoling, smarting under harsh reviews and soliciting favorable ones, suggesting to the poet Robert McAlmon how to phrase his review but McAlmon, tired of being minion, wanted to pursue his own ambitions and was preparing a memoir: *Being Geniuses Together*.

The letters to Frank Budgen and others take on a more austere tone and lewd remarks are no longer tolerated. Regretting an overfrank disclosure which he had written to Budgen, he decided to retrieve it. Budgen was invited to Paris, asked to bring the offending letter and the pair of them went on a night's spree.

Joyce ensured that his friend was the drunker of the two and took Budgen to a bus stop. Next morning Budgen's wallet was delivered to his hotel with the incriminating letter removed. The friendship would never be the same again.

Fame had changed him. What he would say in his books he would conceal in his life. When a drinking companion said, "Here's to sin" Joyce countered with, "I won't drink to that." Nora and he, no longer the rabid lovers, were now called by him "Beati Innocenti." Stanislaus visiting him in Paris found him "too moneyed and pampered," said he drank too much and played with words too much. Nora saw to it that his dress improved—velvet smoking jackets with a silk cravat and instead of an ash plant he carried a snakeskin stick. The old coats and waistcoats were cast aside. The people who surrounded him were there to serve and they took their cue from his moods.

He may have become grander and more remote but he was not a recluse. Arthur Power said that Joyce functioned best in a noisy place. He needed people around him. Unlike Marcel Proust, that other genius who was writing in Paris at the very same time, Joyce avoided the sepulchre. At social gatherings, buoyed with drink, he would remember the advice of a fellow author James Stephens with whom he shared a birthday— "rejoyce and be exceedingly glad." He would sing his favorite song, "Oh, the Brown and the Yellow Ale." He had learned a prettified version of it in the *Irish Homestead* as a youth but had searched for the more bawdy version which dealt with woman's waywardness and man's cuckoldry—a husband going along the road with his married wife is asked by a stranger to lend her for an hour and a day and he agrees to but dies of shame on account of her debauchery. Joyce sang beautifully, his voice charged with feeling, pausing on each note so that to his listeners it was "pure Irish," and filled with "Tenderness, melancholy, bitterness." On these occasions his stiffness and his shyness left him but as the American poet Archibald MacLeish said, there was about him "something vivid and dangerous underneath." His eye surgeon, Dr. Borsch, put it differently; he said Joyce "was a strange fellow but a big Boss."

He could not have lived without outings and appreciation. Isolation would have been unbearable. Many great writers have withdrawn from life as the fear of squandering the inner spark becomes more likely, but Joyce was an exception. His exile was so complete within himself that interruption could not endanger it, only time could do that. Time in which he would begin his "book of the dark," *Finnegans Wake*, a book in which people were not only people, they were as well rivers, bushes, mounds, boundless embodiments of Irish mythological figures, human longings, human impulses caught in an archetypal sweep. New words, phantasmagoric words "breathing in upon his breaking brain."

Joseph Conrad in a letter to a sorrowing aunt wrote "how solitude loses its terrors once one fully knows it" and to a reader one feels that Conrad is speaking truth, but for Joyce solitude would have meant the madhouse. His fear of dogs and thunder are no secret to us, his fear of madness he both admitted and repudiated, but his fear of aloneness he kept to himself. His family were a bulwark against it and so was drink. The exile which had been first from his own country extended to an exile from all of the rest of the world and to endure it he had to have bustle around him. The visitors always gauged their behavior by his mood, his smile or his non-smile. Nora would sit with the guests, not even offering them a drink until Joyce appeared, his blindness adding to the sense of formality as he recognized them by their voices, then took his customary place by the window. The first half hour was always somewhat somber, conversation so stilted that even Miss Weaver who might have traveled from England to assure him of her support was addressed formally. It was not simply grandeur, it was a man with a distance between himself and others. Dublin was his inner landscape with Paris—"that most convenient city"—the place where he found people willing to serve and bolster him. It is said that when he went into a restaurant someone would obligingly jump up and sing "It's a Long Way to Tipperary." In contrast to the salubrious outings, home life was somewhat makeshift. A student of Dr. Borsch's who had been called in an emergency to the apartment found Joyce wrapped in a blanket like a yogi, squatting on the floor, his wife opposite, the carcass of a chicken stew and an empty wine bottle, evidence of their repast. His children, who were by then almost twenty, were recruited in the service of his genius. Blind to their needs at that time as the fate of his book consumed him, Giorgio would be sent around Paris to various bookshops to see how many copies of the second edition of *Ulysses* had sold. Later he tried, then shrank from different occupations and as his life drifted he said it would have been better if he was the "son of a butcher."

Do writers have to be such monsters in order to create? I believe that they do. It is a paradox that while wrestling with language to capture the human condition they become more callous, and cut off from the very human traits which they so glisteningly depict. There can be no outer responsibility, no interruptions, only the ongoing inner drone, rhythmic, insistent, struggling to make a living moment of both beauty and austerity. For Joyce, people were becoming more remote and would eventually be specters. He was not the only one. Flaubert's mother thought that her son's love of words had hardened his heart and all who met Joyce found that though he could be humorous, he lacked warmth. Nora complained of an impossible life, minding a difficult daughter and sitting up with artists till all hours, "bored stiff." "Men," she decreed, "were only up in your tail."

Joyce was lucky to be able to find seclusion and return to a world where Nora was preparing dinner or more often dressing to go out to dinner and telling him to take off "that awful aul jacket." He was luckier than many other writers of the twentieth century, than Osip Mandelstam say, whose obsession with and thralldom for words often remind me of Joyce. Mandelstam like many of the great Russian poets ended up in a concentration camp, his luminous poetry incurring his death. Joyce's torments were different. The strains were beginning to show. He had endocrine treatment for his arthritis, had to have all his teeth removed and was fitted with permanent plates. His eyesight so worsened that he had only one-seventh normal vision. He was given dionine leeches for his bad eye but soon it was clear that they would have to operate.

A coolness arose with Miss Beach. Ironically it was over *Ulysses*. She wrote to tell him that by allowing a second edition of *Ulysses* to be published she was in danger of being brought up before a French court for having palmed off a first bogus edition. Angry booksellers, angry publishers and angry collectors were all threatening her. It was their first breach but it foreshadowed a greater one. Joyce continued to avail himself of her services as secretary and publicist and both he and Nora felt that they could borrow on future royalties from her till. It was left to Adrienne Monnier, who was by now her lover, to write and tell him what she had for a long time been meditating on.

Miss Beach, his "maid of all work," was being exploited. They had been put upon, they had been made to hustle, Shakespeare & Co. had existed only for the benefit of James Joyce. Those who thought Joyce indifferent to fame and fortune were sadly mistaken, as she could assure them. True to his dissimulating nature he did not enter the fray. He said that it was always best not to act oneself, to cultivate ostensible aloofness and to pull strings.

"I am always friends with a person for a purpose," he had said, and Miss Beach's purpose was waning. He would replace her with another acolyte. He had found in the quiet Miss Weaver a more generous, more serene and more stalwart friend. At the very height of his defection, he even wrote to Miss Beach to say that no doubt she would be glad to hear that Miss Weaver had given him the "very great gift of another £12,000"—a brusque way of telling her she was dethroned.

Miss Weaver

MISS WEAVER, the daughter of staunch Church of England parents, was instrumental in having episodes of *A Portrait of the Artist* serialized in *The Egoist*, an avant-garde magazine which she coedited. Her first approach to him has a Cinderella tentativeness. From her capital, which was not vast, she fixed a regular sum for Joyce to draw each month and chose to do it anonymously through a firm of solicitors. Joyce and Nora were agog to know who this fairy godmother was and Joyce guessed that it was a woman because the donor had been moved "by his piercing style." When the secret became known Miss Weaver apologized for having embarrassed him. His extravagance, his drinking, his Croesus-like need for greater and greater sums would loom, but by the time she saw these profligate habits there was no turning back. She was his savior, remaining deaf to the petty cavils of those who insisted that her patronage had given him freedom to write an unintelligible book. She endured the wrath of her solicitors who did not understand her rashness and the sneers of friends who wondered at her indulgence. Over the years she dug into her own capital, lived frugally and even feared that she would have to sell her flat to go on supporting him. True to a long line of dauntless Englishwomen who risked their lives and their respectability for a "cause," Miss Weaver found her cause in the person of James Augustine

Aloysius Joyce. That she loved him was undoubted and that it was never even broached is remarkable. Whenever she received a small pension from this or that deceased relative, she rushed to put it at his disposal. When from Paris he voiced his concern over worsening impecunity she would cross the Channel to reassure him of her support. She saw him down bottle after bottle of wine, tip lavishly, travel by taxi when she herself traveled by bus, but it did nothing to disillusion her. When on a visit to Torquay James and Nora stayed in the Imperial Hotel he arranged with the manager to give his patron a special rate and felt himself to be the chevalier in her life.

Various estimates have been made of how much Miss Weaver gave him, and in the equivalent of today's currency it is thought to be close to a million dollars. She asked for nothing in return. This was not Sylvia Beach who wanted a share in the glory or the imperious Mrs. Harold (Edith Rockefeller) McCormick, who took up causes and soon tired of her philanthropy. This was the quiet unassuming spinster born to alleviate the troubles of a man "baffled, beaten, vanquished and pulverized," as he put it. Her original intention was to give him pause to write but soon her role extended to help with his living expenses, his wife's living expenses, his children's needs, their illnesses, his numerous eye operations, the hotels in Paris where he lived, and the more opulent hotels where he vacationed.

Their relationship was mostly by letter and when they met all the formalities were maintained—she being Miss Weaver and he being Mr. Joyce. She is the embodiment of Kierkegaard's ideal in *Purity of Heart* where the labor and sacrifice is for the thing itself and not to glorify the giver. His letters to her are the most confiding of all. They changed as he himself changed. The early letters to Stanislaus helped him to define his intellectual and political aspirations, indulge his arrogance and describe himself as a socialist, by which he meant that he expected to be supported by the State. His letters to Nora are the playful ones of their courtship days and the ravenously sexual ones dispatched from his father's house in Fontenoy Street when he was still a young man. Those to Miss Weaver while being shot with humor are full of gravity and depletion and in one he confessed that he had not read a work of literature in several years and that his head was full of pebbles and rubble and broken matches and lots of glass "picked up most everywhere." They began politely, expressions of courtesy and gratitude for what she had done, but soon came the predictable requests for books and gramophone records, press cuttings, a harrying of this editor or that, to use an extract of his work, and unquestioning admiration for what he was writing. His dependence veered from the financial to the emotional and then back again to the financial.

She behaved flawlessly. She never judged, never rebuked, and not once overstepped her role. Joyce, particularly as he got older, was a formal man and to this equally formal woman he could confide the several things which racked and rent him. She was told everything: the family doings, the incessant house huntings, the rashers and eggs he ate on a train journey, the new jacket of green stuff he bought in Salzburg and the silk handkerchief and sombrero he acquired to go with it. Then it was his oculist or his dentist, his iritis, the abscesses in his gums, the doses to his nebula and every other peradventure of his turbulent life. As they grew closer his need of money became more rapacious. Sometimes he hinted and sometimes he asked outright. She is about to go on holiday and with some sense of propriety, he wishes her a pleasant stay, then launches into the grim reality of his treasury sucked up by some giant vacuum which he omitted to call "himself." Could she ensure that the money which was to come on such-and-such a date arrive sooner? Not only that, but could he draw on the capital rather than on the promised monthly sum? She never found the hardness of heart to say no. In a parting shot of humor after one or other of these plaints, he said that he expected she would be relieved not to meet him on a platform with an eyepatch and a list of impossible requests. She had become friend, confidante, confessor, and all-forgiving mother.

She did however get something in return. She was to see the wonder of his imagination in flight, his "passencore" and his "wielderfight"of words. She was sent the keys to his fabulous kingdom, hints of meaning for his linguistic distortions and his Oconees. As he began to write *Finnegans Wake*, he sent glossary after glossary, tables of explanation and little nudges for her to delight in his word puzzles. "Wolkencap" was a woolen cap of clouds, "dinn" was an oriental mixture of din and djinn.

"Life is a wake . . . live it or crick it." One morning in Paris, despite upheavals, failing eyesight, and poor health Joyce took a notebook with foolscap paper and commenced on his *Work in Progress*, the title of which he jealously guarded, confiding it only to Nora in case he died. It would, of course, be *"Finnegans Wake—Live It or Crick It."* *"Ulysses*—who wrote it, I've forgotten," he said. If *Ulysses* was a book about daytime, *Finnegans Wake* was a book of the night. Dream and riddle, mythmaking, myth breaking, syllepses, syllogisms, naturalism, supernaturalism, fabulism, kings and giants along with Sir Tristram, violer d'amores, and Anna Livia with her "rhunerhinerstones" and her seven rainbow handmaids. He thought it the strongest stuff he had ever written but he also guessed that the book would be the death of him. Already he felt himself to be both man and ghost and a ghost he had described as one who has faded into impalpability, through death, through absence, through change of manners.

He was laying siege to literature, ensuring "a nice little attack of brain ache" on his readers. Art was to move on to reveal ideas and formless spiritual essences, the old language was to be put to sleep. Words would be broken down to extract the substance from them, "water would speak like water, birds chirrup like birds" as he freed language from its erstwhile servile, contemptible role. The ports of call not known beforehand. Words spliced, added to and compounded to have a denser meaning. The boudoir for instance, where Anna Livia with the help of her seven rainbow girls braids her hair, was converted to boudelaire, a meshing of bou for mud and a deference to Baudelaire.

The first two exuberant pages which he sent her dealt with the fate of Roderick O'Conor, the last High King of Ireland: *I've a terrible errible lot todue todie todue tooterribleday*, well, what did he go and do at all, His Most Exuberant Majesty King Roderick O'Conor but, arrah bedamnbut, he finalised by lowering his woolly throat with the wonderful midnight thirst was on him, as keen as mustard, he could not tell what he did ale, that bothered he was from head to tail, and, wishawishawish, leave it, what the Irish, boys, can do, if he did'nt go, sliggymag

looral reemyround and suck up, sure enough, like a Trojan, in some particular cases with the assistance of his venerated tongue, whatever surplus rotgut, sorra much, was left by the lazy lousers of maltknights and beerchurls in the different bottoms of the various different replenquished drinking utensils left there behind them on the premises by that whole hogsheaded firkin family . . ." The Roderick O'Conor of history was a more robust and warring fellow who ruled a small principality in stony Connaught and naturally aspired to be High King of all Ireland. His chance came when the High King McLochlann took a hostage from Ulster and blinded him. In a century and a culture noted for its barbarity, blinding was nevertheless thought to be sacrilege and the High King was thus deserted by his loyal followers and slain near Armagh. Roderick marched through three provinces, had himself crowned as High King, only to be later toppled echoing the line in Jan Kott's *Shakespeare Our Contemporary*—"the King is dead, long live the King."

Joyce would send Miss Weaver installments as he wrote them and with uncustomary humility suggested that she pick a theme of her choice and he would deliver it with the same alacrity as a tailor might deliver a suit or a baker a loaf of bread. He needed her and he would need her more as episodes appeared in magazines incurring the wrath of friends and foes. It was denounced as being "chopsuey, a legpull, a vast riddle and an assault on commonsense." Nobody could follow it. What most of us do in sleep Joyce was attempting to do in his waking hours. It would isolate him completely—"his heart's adrone, his bluidstreams acrawl, his puff but a piff."

The Wake

ULYSSES HE HAD made out of next to nothing but _Finnegans Wake_ he was "making out of nothing at all, with thunderbolts in it." A book of the night, he described it as a mountain which he tunneled into from two directions not knowing what he would find. It was a case of more maps, more encyclopedias, more street directories, but this time, the arena was the world although dear old doublin Dublin would be the principal locale. Myth and transubstantiation, giants and humans would incarnate into one another and eventually be converted into trees or cloud or rivers. Rivers dominate the narrative, eight hundred in all—Mississippi and Missouri, "seepy and sewery"—but most of all the River Liffey "from swerve of shore to bend of bay, brings us by a commodious vicus recirculation back to Howth Castle."

Howth was the burial place of Finn MacCool, the giant Irish hero whose frame was so vast that his head was in one place, his belly somewhere else and his feet in Phoenix Park. Finn MacCool, progenitor of Bygmister Tim Finnegan, the "hazeydency" hod carrier. Howth was also the most vulnerable point of Dublin Bay being open to invasion from foreigners. Bygmester Joyce was himself soon to suffer the assault of critics and even stalwarts for this "verbal acupuncture."

While years later Joseph Campbell would describe *Finnegans Wake* as "Fructifying mother Ireland with the gyzm of the eternal" and Fred Higginson would speak of Joyce's "Breugelesque prodigality," in his time he was ridiculed as "Shem the Penman" with the "gift of the garbage." It was all very well for Joyce to call it on occasion a "jetsam of litterage" or a "loquacity of any way words" but when others made the same judgments he retaliated. He said it was so simple that anyone could understand it. The real heroes were time, the river, and the mountain; man and woman, birth, childhood, night sleep, marriage, prayer and death. He was trying as he said to build a narrative on many planes but with a single aesthetic purpose. But between what he said and what he did there were "moyles and moyles" of difference.

He worked with either one or two eyes and had repeated doses of cocaine to relieve the pain. He worked at night and laughed so loudly at his own "bauchspeech" that Nora would get up and tell him to stop writing and stop laughing so that she could get a bit of sleep. Sometimes the absorption was such that he lost consciousness. Between two words he might insert two hundred more and a single page would extend to twenty or thirty pages. But the avalanche of language was too much.

Oliver Gogarty called it the "most colossal legpull since Macpherson's *Ossian*" in which that author claimed to have received psychic communications from the dead. Gogarty had waited almost thirty years to wreak his revenge, a revenge founded on nothing more or less than that they were contemporaries in Dublin, both writers, the one a genius, the other a satirist. His essay has all the bile and malice which the lesser talent reserves for the greater, or in Anna Livia's words—"[A]ll the greed gushes out through their small souls." According to

Gogarty, Joyce's mind was hardly consistent with sanity. He concluded his epitaph with the (false) hope that the indiscriminate adulation which Joyce was receiving from the literary dilettantes of Paris would soothe a heart insatiable for fame. If *Ulysses* had angered people, this new work would send them into paroxysms.

So what is it? A maze of "discinct and isoplural" words born in the "blotchwall of his innkempt house," a deuteronomy. "Outer serpumstances" are given short shrift. Each reader has to make a daring leap to construe meaning and of course laughter. "Latin me that, my trinity scholard" says one of the gabbling washerwomen to another, while their author strove to turn "sanscreed into oure eryan!" If Ireland thought she had a defector in James Joyce, she was greatly mistaken. Her music, poetry and "broken heaventalk" are all there.

Bygmester Finnegan, gammer and gaffer, while working on a "skyerscape" one "thirstay mournin" slipped and fell. Mr. Finnegan, transmuting into the person of Humphrey Chimpden Earwicker, owns a public house in Chapelizod, has a wife Anna Livia, rival twins Shem and Shaun, and their sister Isabel, she with the split personality, an Iseult in search of her Tristan. Mr. and Mrs. Everyman with human hopes, human aspirations and all too human frailties dwarfed by nature or converted to mere lisps of speech.

Anna Livia is the most accessible and indeed beloved character ever conceived by Joyce. She is living woman who sheds the garments of youth, then the garments of age leaf by leaf, as she returns to her first abode, her "cold mad feary father" the waiting sea. He called it his "melodic" chapter and even the hardest hearts and minds were moved. The French critic Valery Larbaud was in a trance over it. It was published separately and to encourage readers Joyce composed a little limerick for the limited edition.

> Buy a book in brown paper
> From Faber and Faber
> To see Annie Liffey trip, tumble and caper.
> Sevensinns in her singthings,
> Plurabells on her prose
> Seashell ebb music wayriver she flows.

In Book I, Chapter 5, Anna is described by two washer-women gossiping by a river, stooping and steeping the sin and the stains out of the dirty torn clothing they have been hired to wash. Each one is egging the other on to tell about Anna and in franca lingua at that, to "call a spate a spate." O you'll die when you hear. Anna was "licked by a hound, Chirripa-Chirruta, while doing her pee, pure and simple, on the spur of the hill in old Kippure, in birdsong and shearingtime, but first of all, worst of all, the wiggly livvly, she sideslipped out by a gap in the Devil's glen while Sally her nurse was sound asleep in a sloot and, feefee fiefie, fell over a spillway before she found her stride and lay and wriggled in all the stagnant black pools of rainy under a fallow coo," and worse still, procured for her husband, "His Affluence," the dirty dumpling, the services of young girls, playthings to sit on his lap. Her husband is a bumpkin. Wasn't he caught in the fiendish Phoenix Park doing a terrible thing, getting girls—"gigglibly temptatrixes"—to undress so as for him to indulge in improper acts like passing water or worse and this in front of three swaggering soldier boys. Wasn't the disgrace conveyed in a ballad that fluttered throughout Ireland on a handkerchief. Deliverance comes many puzzles and many ramifications later. A letter, brought to light

by the hen Belinda when scratching on a heap of dirt and when
held up to the sunlight, is seen to have been gashed and
pierced with a pronged instrument. Nevertheless the intention
is to clear the character of the scallywag husband. He had to
see life foully—"the plak and the smut" of it, he had to have
his fill of the apple harlots. It may be that it is Anna, the all-
forgiving wife and water mother who has written the letter, a
vindication of Bygmester Finnegan, Humphrey Earwicker and
Dane Dodderer.

Anna does, in the end, ask if there is "one who under-
stands" her but in her youth she too was part of the wild dance
and the wild din. Whereas Molly is all appetite, Anna is incan-
tatory. She is an apparition of winding coils, a fugitive en-
chantress who washes herself with galawater and with leaf
mold dries her "round prunella isles and eslets dun," her
"quincecunct" and her "little mary." Her hair may have been
inspired by Livia Schmitz's but it is metamorphosed into mead-
owgrass, riverflags, bulrush, waterweed and weeping willow.
We stay with her when she plaits it. In time her desire for
Humperfeldt wanes. The bedchamber grows solemn. He locks
his "kekkle" up. She will be given second place to their daughter Iseult, the Issy of Chapelizod whom the husband-father cov-
ets as his daughter-wife. The mossiness of the mother is soon to
be replaced by "whisk brisk sly spry spink" of a daughter.

Edmund Wilson said of *Finnegans Wake* that in it husband
and wife will waken from their night's sleep with a new polar-
ization. The father, Mr. Wilson says, is pulling toward the children and the wife withdrawing from her husband, the lecher,
not however in rancor but in compassion. Anna closes her eyes
to see him as "a child beside a weenywhite steed," the child
every mother likes to believe in. Transformed into a river, she

has to pass on her way through their "therrble prongs" of South Wall and North Wall before being taken into the wide sea. Her last words an incantation—"A way a lone a last a loved a long the" The critic William York Tindall called this "purest schmalz," as if to write about meeting death could be so demeaned.

Joyce had always thought that the faithful Miss Weaver would not desert him. She had, after all, been sent into his life through the ministering spirit of Homer since her name suggested Penelope's weaving and unweaving of the tapestry. He was mistaken. His "integuments" as they were called were too much and Miss Weaver began to get cold feet. She did not like the outpourings from his wholesale pun factory and she did not like the unintelligibility of it. "Do you not like anything I write?" he asked her. She liked the waterworld and the ghostliness. Ghostliness there was in plenty.

"Grey starr, green starr, black starr, nocturnal starr." Near blind from the deposits in his eyes, writing with different-colored pens, the lettering half an inch thick, he felt himself brother to "the fierce indignation" of Dean Swift. Ezra Pound said, ". . .[N]othing short of divine vision or a new cure for the clapp can possibly be worth all the circumambient peripherization."

Joyce was all alone. The intricacy, the binding together of sound, semi-sound and image to make his weirdly beautiful word constellations was too much. While writing it he pored over the workmanship of the tunc pages of *The Book of Kells* not only because of their intricate illuminated designs but because they told the story of the Gospel. He believed that he was doing the same. He had said that the idea for the book came from Vico's *Scienza nuova*, the use of ethnology and mythology to uncover important events, destruction and recurrence of human history always repeating itself—"The seim anew." But once he started on it Vico's theory was a "mere trellis." His mind into which everything had to be crammed was "a transparent leaf away from madness."

The telephone wires which he saw through a manhole in the street resembled navel cords and the flowers which he had been told of in the ruins of Carthage became the lilts of dead children. His inspiration for the hair of Anna Livia was the beautiful red hair of Livia Schmitz (wife of his friend Italo Svevo) but it was also the River Dartry streaked red from the empty canisters thrown out from the nearby dye works. At a bazaar he sighted a Turk with a framework on his knees and the skeins of red, green, blue and yellow thread he saw as a split rainbow. The magic of early Irish fable his daily bread. He would have relished the story of the saint who, walking upon the sea, met Barra in his ship and Barra asked how it was that the saint could walk upon the water, only to be told, "It is not sea at all that I am on but a flowery blossomy field." The saint then plucked a crimson flower and tossed it to Barra in the ship, then asked how it was that a ship could float upon a field and Barra stretched his hand down deep and took a salmon up out of the water.

Land and water, image and counterimage, the oaks of old rising out of the ashes of time to create "yonder elm" and above all Dublin and its outskirts reinvented in breathtaking vignettes. Edgar Quinet, whom he admired, was paid the honor of having a piece of his prose ceremoniously moved from Illyria and Numantia to the environs of Dublin—"the cornflowers have been staying at Ballymun, the duskrose has choosed out Goatstown's hedges, twolips have pressed togatherthem by sweet Rush, townland of twinedlights, the whitethorn and the redthorn have fairygeyed the mayvalleys of Knockmaroon . . . fresh and made-of-all smiles as, on the eve of Killallwho."

As the work appeared in "instorments" in literary magazines, the furor intensified. The book was "linguistic sodomy," the work of "a ship-wrecked mind incapable of delivering its cargo."

Twelve helpmates, or "apostles" as he called them, were summoned each to write an article so as to make people "ontherstand" the impossible work. Overseen, and sometimes dictated to by Joyce, the apostles included Frank Budgen, Samuel Beckett, Stuart Gilbert, Robert McAlmon and others, all of them expatiating on its prelingual symbolism, its aqueous influences, its riparian geography, the facts of its being "conical rather than spherical"; written in a language "drunk, tilted and effervescent." Another glaring example of the ongoing mistake of trying to explain or dissect a single line of James Joyce. He loathed literary conversation and said he would rather talk about turnips but he was wise now to the fact of the bombast and falsehood of the literary and academic sensibilities. He knew that these essays would incite tremendous interest, as they did. They are marvels of ponderousness, abstraction and opaqueness, and ultimately irksome.

He admitted to wanting to keep the critics busy for the next three hundred years. Yet at Fouquet's restaurant in Paris with a childlike hesitation he asked his daughter-in-law, Helen, to read a passage which he had just written and which next day he expanded from two pages to ten. No explanation needed of Vico's theory (which the apostles had rambled on about) or the resemblance to Dante's "purgatorial process," only the sheer thrill of hearing—"Soft morning, city! I am leafy speafing. Folty and folty all the nights have been falling on to long my hair. Not a sound falling. The woods are so fond always. It is for my golden wedding. Rise up, man of the hooths . . ."

Paul Léon describes Joyce as listening with evident and intense pleasure and saying quite earnestly that maybe after all he might not have to look for a job as a street singer. His despair when writing *Finnegans Wake* was such that he even thought of asking James Stephens to finish it and another time began an aborted scheme to enlist for a teaching post in Cape Town. The leaps in his mood from arrogance to ingenuousness are probably what made so many people enlist as his slave and prompted Samuel Beckett to say after his death that he was "a very lovable human being." Beckett and himself had grown somewhat estranged as time went on. At first Beckett's worship of the master was such that he wore the same size shoes even though he had larger feet, smoked the same cigarettes and lolled on a chair in the same manner as Joyce did, but when his "voluntary services" as occasional secretary swelled, he took flight. Joyce always put his friends, and particularly his errant friends, into his work and Beckett is given a somewhat equivocal encomium—"Sam knows miles bettern me how to work the miracle. And I see by his diarrhio he's droppin the stammer out of his silenced bladder since I bonded him off more as a friend and as a brother."

Into this *Work in Progress* Joyce crammed everything, the "Fistic Styles" of boxers, the "silent O'Moyle Waters," Christy Colomba, Brendan the Navigator, Bruno, Cassio, squawking seagulls and Bartholoman's Deep somewhere in Chile. But it was *"Trappo Grossa San Giacomone."* The English critic Desmond

McCarthy said Joyce was determined to write "as a lunatic for lunatics." What he was determined to do was to break the barrier between conscious and unconscious, to do in waking life what others do in sleep. Madness he knew to be the secret of genius. Hamlet was mad in his opinion and it was that madness which induced the great drama. The characters in the Greek plays were mad and so was Gogol and so was Van Gogh. He preferred the word "exaltation" which can merge into madness. All great men had that vein in them. The reasonable man, he insisted, achieves nothing.

In a rare moment of candor he said to Miss Weaver, "Perhaps I shall survive, perhaps the raving madness I write will survive and perhaps it is funny." Behind this doubt and barely concealed despair was a deeper and more desperate hope that "the fire of madness kindling" in Lucia's brain "would die out."

"When I leave this dark night she will be cured" was his one consolation to himself during the seventeen-year labor of his "cruelfiction." As always for him, life and work had a secret and magical corollary. By drowning Vincent Cosgrave in *Ulysses* Joyce believed that he had precipitated Cosgrave's own drowning and in the same occult way he would bring Lucia back from the brink.

Kith and Kin

AT FORTY-NINE Joyce reached life's nadir. Three irreparable things had happened to him: his father's death, the world's indifference to *Finnegans Wake* and Lucia's askew and fragmenting psyche.

When John Joyce, aged eighty-two, died in the Christmas of 1931, James sank into a Lear-like state of lamentation, blaming himself for a decade of near neglect and occasional outbursts of cruelty. Waves of guilt and bathos possessed him as he recalled his father's great gifts and lonely widowhood, or as John had put it, "Cast upon the wretched heartless world without one relative to give food or shelter." In the days before John's death, he had sent letters, wires, telephoned the hospital each evening and importuned a friend, Curran, to visit his father and keep him up to date with the news. On hearing of the death he broke down and blamed himself for not having secured the best medical specialist.

John, who had been delirious for some days, rallied on his deathbed and his last words were: "Tell Jim he was born at six in the morning." True to his promise, he left all his worldly goods to his favorite son but what Joyce had always wanted was praise for his work. His family, like his countrymen, had withheld that, thereby amplifying Yeats's precept—

Edna O'Brien

Out of Ireland have we come.
Great hatred, little room,
Maimed us at the start.

Over the years John Joyce had written plaintive letters vowing that each communiqué would be his last, which of course it wasn't. Dejection, poverty, a man abandoned by his daughters, despised, rejected, jeered at and hated. The only person who could help him was Jim and after the publication of *Ulysses* when Joyce became world-renowned his father felt entitled to some of the spoils. Joyce's reply comes as a bitter disappointment from a man who was not only to dissolve at the news of his father's death but who was also to accuse himself for the rest of his life for having failed that stranded father. His refusal was categoric. It was true, he conceded, that he was receiving a monthly allowance from an English lady but most of that was spent on rent, medical bills and a cleaning woman. He omitted to list their extravagances, Nora's penchant for expensive clothes and their almost nightly excursions to famous restaurants in Paris which Hemingway ruefully confessed were beyond his means. To assure his father of his own hardships he said that he made the beds in the morning, stoked the stove and that their apartment was so dark that he had difficulty finding his clothes.

A master at rebuke he was however, ten years later, reduced to a state of wounded infant-like despair. He confided his prone state to his friends and wrote to the marmoreal T. S. Eliot of the intensity of his father's love for him. Remorse about not returning to Ireland resurfaced with the oblique allusion to the "instinct" which held him back. His resistance to Ireland was something beyond fear, it was a pathology. His given reason, along with an abhorrence for his work, treacherous friends and pusillanimous publishers, was that he would be lynched by his own, killed just as his hero Parnell had been killed. He never failed to recall the drama which befell Nora and the children when in 1922 they had visited Galway and were made to lie on the floor of a train because of an exchange of shells between Republicans and Free State soldiers. There was carnage all over Europe but for Joyce, Ireland was the primal battlefield, "Bludefilth."

His communications with his father had been sporadic. He would ask friends when visiting Dublin to call on the poor man and bring him a bottle of Jameson's whiskey. He had had a portrait done which he kept in his study along with the Joyce coat of arms and his father's embroidered hunting coat. John had once suggested he might come to visit them, pitifully adding that of course he would pay his own way and his own lodgings. The visit never materialized.

In this his dark hour Joyce was no longer the world-famous, haughty, revered author, he was a son "thanking from his heart" Curran who had visited the father in Drumcondra hospital. To Miss Weaver he wrote not only of his prostration of mind but his decision to abandon *Finnegans Wake*, to leave the pages "unfinished with blanks." His relationship with this father would be forever unfinished, pre-empting the world's relationship with this "wildering book of the dark." He wrote to her of his father's wit, wet and dry, his little sillinesses, his shrewdness, his host of stories, claiming that his father's genius had informed hundreds of pages and scores of characters in *Ulysses*.

For the funeral he sent a wreath of ivy in commemoration of his own and his father's love for Parnell. The accompanying card said "Sorrow and Love from Jim," as if they two alone constituted the family tree. Miss Weaver, mother, grandmother and fairy godmother to the Joyce clan, was approached by Padraic Colum to assist with the funeral expenses, which of course she did.

The sum of six hundred and sixty-five pounds, nine shillings and no pence which had been willed to James was swallowed up by debts and hospital expenses. He didn't mind. His father had proved his love for him and in atonement he assumed a symbiotic closeness; his father's voice had got inside his own throat and his father's way of sighing would now be his. He even thought that the dead man was trying to talk to him and wondered as he had never wondered before about the next world.

"Father, if ever I take a fancy to anybody, I swear to you on the head of Jesus that it will not be because I am not fond of you. Do not forget that." It was how Lucia wrote to her father, depending on him as she did to shepherd her through.

Long before he had expressed a fear that a malady had taken possession of his children when they lived in Switzerland. He never defined this malady but with Nora and himself so sexually besotted and his work so consuming the children were somewhat relegated. In her teens he came to love Lucia unreservedly, she was his "inspiratrice" and her derangement merely an expression of her genius derouted.

Her childhood, like her brother's, had been fitful—different schools, different private tutors, a hotchpotch of languages and a chronic shortage of money intermixed with bouts of extravagance. Lucia, who resembled her mother and even had the same slight squint, had also inherited Nora's stroppiness. As a youngster she would complain that her brother and herself were locked like "pigs in a sty" when her father and mother went to a restaurant or to the opera. Giorgio was her ally and when in time he became engaged to an American heiress, Helen Fleischman, Lucia's wild words for her rival was that she was "the gigolo."

Joyce believed that his genius had cast its shadow on Lucia's psyche and perhaps it had. But his guilt reeks of something darker and more incriminating, and as if her malady was not the consequence of his genius but his early youthful dissipation. The sins of the fathers. Samuel Beckett when he met her saw the father's mind running rampant in the daughter. He thought she was like a charmed snake, cut off from those around her and with a longing to create. She resented her mother, would shout at her and say she was sex-starved, in short, Joyce-starved. A slender, dark-haired girl with brilliant blue eyes, she was so highly strung that her conversations would skid from one topic to another. Beckett was first drawn to her because of this acceleration but soon began to feel alarmed over her growing attachment to him. He saw that she was going insane but said that no one else saw it, especially her besotted father. Beckett had sat with Joyce at the Bal Bullien watching Lucia dance in a shimmering silver fish costume, Joyce chafing when she was not awarded first place and putting it down to a vogue for Negroid dancing. Not having succeeded at that she decided to quit dancing, took to her bed for days, then poured all her energies into the conquest of Beckett. She would wait for him inside the door, arrange lunches in restaurants, while he resorted to the male strategy of evading her affections by bringing a friend along. At one of these lunches her disappointment was so great that she stared into space, ate nothing, cried, then ran out leaving two penniless would-be poets confronted with the bill. For Beckett her feelings were not only too overt, they were, as he put it, "like incest." When he told her frankly that it was her father whom he came to see, she lapsed into one of her catatonic states, adding this failure to so many others. She had studied singing, drawing, and seventeen different kinds of dancing but was a helpless, floundering girl with no man to pay court to her, only her father. Nora blamed Beckett for his advances and he was barred from visiting the family.

At Joyce's fifty-third birthday party she threw a chair at her mother and George had to hold her down as two orderlies strapped her into a straitjacket. Her father, helpless to do anything, watched her being carried out to an ambulance. Within days she discharged herself but Nora was in dread of being alone with her ever again. Her father refused to concede that she might be mad and said she was just a young girl who was "prey to sudden impulses." Joyce was not afraid of madness. It was a word he often used, just as his father used it when asked what he thought of Jim's work. But madness on the page is one thing, madness in the other room is quite another. There was Lucia either sitting listlessly by a window, or throwing furniture at her mother and hurling abuse, saying her mother had made her a bastard by not having been married when she was born. Her father was absolved from any wrongdoing.

He would grudgingly consent to have her see this doctor or that, to have her admitted to a sanatorium and then, regretting it, he would smuggle her out. She refused to see any more psychiatrists and several friends in Paris were summoned as her guardian. The degree to which Joyce indulged her temper is outstanding. When for instance she was staying with Mary Colum, wife of the Irish poet, the doctor was instructed to pretend that it was Mrs. Colum he was examining and Lucia merely there as a guest. She and Mrs. Colum slept with their two nightgown sleeves pinned together but nevertheless Lucia bolted. She made no secret of the fact that she was looking for a man. Joyce even admitted that she had had men friends but said somewhat cavalierly that he did not mind being a "vieillard" as her suitors were mere "striplings." The ugly rumor was that they had had a sexual relationship but Joyce loved her too much for that and her love of him has in it the intensity of Greek tragedy. He was everything to her. She wanted him reconciled to his own country, she wrote to the King of England to acknowledge her father's genius and no matter how rash her claims, Joyce simply said, "Hear, hear." For all her derangements he had an explanation, insisting it was physical and not psychic. He grudgingly approved of this or that cure, took her to this or that doctor and he even surrendered his own misgivings and brought her to see Jung whom he had dismissed as the tweedledum of Zurich because Jung had been so dense about *Ulysses*. At first Jung thought he could cure her but then abandoned the hope and saw them as two people at the bottom of a pool, one diving and one drowning. She, for her part, called him "a big fat materialistic Swiss man" who was trying to get a hold on her soul. Joyce thought everything she said to be perspicacious and admired her for being, like himself, unsparing in her "lightning-lit reveries." Even when he saw that she had drawn a picture of him, a coffin, with the rubric "this is Jim" he was not alarmed. He was losing friends who tried to talk sense to him and inevitably he was losing her.

On his fifty-second birthday, as congratulations poured in and the news that *Ulysses* had at last been published in the United States, she cut the telephone wires twice and struck her mother. So it was on to another clinic, this cure that cure, opposing diagnoses as to what was the matter with her, Joyce buoying her up with letters and that old panacea a promise of a fur coat. Having given up dancing she took up a career of illuminated lettering and he encouraged her in this, believing, as he said to Miss Weaver, that she was not Cézanne but determined that her life should have some point.

Somewhere in the thick of all these aberrations, drugged with laudanum or Veronal, Lucia announced that she wished to be married and favored a July wedding. Her mother and brother thought it complete nonsense but Joyce was in favor. His secretary Paul Léon managed to persuade his brother-in-law Alex Ponisovsky to propose to her and with understandable reluctance the young man did. She accepted readily. Joyce was heartened. All would be well. Friends were nudged to send bouquets and messages of congratulations. Joyce arranged an engagement party which ended in doom. She left the restaurant, went to the Léons' flat and lay prone on a sofa for several days. She called off the engagement, reinstated it, broke it off again within twenty-four hours because she hated all Jews.

Believing that a change of scene and a change of country might do wonders, Joyce wrote to Miss Weaver to ask if Lucia would be welcome in London. The several cures had misfired; ingestions of seawater had not worked and he balked at committing her to an institution from which she would never escape. As with Mary Colum, Miss Weaver found her charge elusive and also had to sleep beside her and hold on to her hand. Yet she managed to escape. Seeing the name Windsor on a bus, Lucia jumped on it, then rang from a hotel to ask Miss Weaver to come immediately and bring a change of clothing. She had absconded before her rescuer arrived. Deciding then that London was not to her liking she settled on Dublin so that she could reconcile that bitter city to the great name of her father. For her Dublin cousins she generated havoc, took an overdose, placed an advertisement in an evening paper for Chinese lessons, went out without underwear and propositioned men that she took a liking to. When she made a fire in her bedroom she said it was because she liked the smell of turf and the red of the fire reminded her of her father's face.

His letters to her are indeed the letters of a lover. In each one he is enclosing money, or a good tonic or a beautiful story by Tolstoy. He is reminding her to take plenty of eggs, milk and fruit and he is pleased to hear that she has found the beige stockings that were always her favourite color. He is father, doctor and wooer. He is recalling a party to which they once went where there were "little lanterns scattered on the grass," the enthralled child in him reaching to the child in her. She was not mad, she was simply using a curious abbreviated language of her own, the one he had developed in *Finnegans Wake*. The Dublin visit ended with her having to be committed to a hospital in Finglas and Joyce, outraged by this, bitterly blamed his sister and nieces and broke with them forever. So it was back to Miss Weaver.

Miss Weaver rented a cottage in Kingswood near Reigate in Surrey and also the services of "a stalwart mental nurse." They took turns watching Lucia and at times when the outbursts were too great, they had to hold her down. When Joyce was told this, he was outraged. His daughter did not need "policing." It meant the nurse had to go. Moreover, he rebuked Miss Weaver for mentioning his daughter in the same breath as his sister or her cousins. Possibly, not having been brought up as a slave and having neither Bolshevik nor Hitlerite tendencies, Lucia was not to everyone's liking and he challenged Miss Weaver to tell him candidly whether or not she liked this daughter of his.

"[I]t is I who am mad," he said, goading her to agree or disagree, and then poured scorn on "the metal money" he was receiving from her.

Lucia's condition deteriorated as the weeks went on and a Dr. MacDonald who believed in "corporeal chastisement" was called in. Very soon he had her admitted to a hospital in Northampton and Joyce lost faith in Miss Weaver's offices and all English and Scottish doctors. He arranged for Lucia to be brought back to a nursing home in Paris which he could visit, still believing that he could save her.

Miss Weaver pleaded to come to Paris to clear up any misunderstanding that might have arisen between them, wanting to visit Lucia and bring a suitcase which she had left behind. Getting no reply she wrote again to remind him that her house number had been changed to 101, a number which she hoped Mr. Joyce would like since it signified the wheel going round. The reply from his secretary, Paul Léon, was formality itself. "Weighty and tragic events" were worrying Mr. Joyce, whom she had failed in the absolute trust which he expected from friends. From then on it was Joyce and Lucia buffeting against the outside world.

Gradually, he began to see the hopelessness of things as Lucia's stays in each Maison de Santé grew longer and her mind veered from babble to haughty grandeur. Her admirers, she said, had all been spurned by her, because all of them including Beckett were Jews. Night now. Night forever.

When in one of her letters she wrote to him and said, "[I]f ever I should go away, it would be to a country which belongs to you . . ." he must have felt the ghost of Anna Livia talking back to him from the page. She did go away. She retreated into the stranglehold of her own mind. Yet when she was told of his death she reacted not as loving daughter but as avenging fury: "What is he doing under the ground, that idiot? When will he decide to come out?" Abandonment.

Himself and Others

HOW JOYCE SAW HIMSELF and how others saw him differed vastly. When one day in Paris Arthur Power said, "You are a man without feelings," Joyce turned, nettled, and said, "My God—I a man without feelings." His bearing was aloof and somewhat aristocratic, his manner slightly ceremonious, his reddish-brown hair upstanding and his lips thin and scornful.

People were afraid of him. He might say to Nora, "Do you see the simplicity behind all my disguises?" but he wore many masks and he could change them sleekly. Some said that he sucked the energy from everything around him, he himself said that he wanted his imagination to grow when he was with people, otherwise it was a case of silence. These "emanations of silence and love" Beckett saw as the secret of Joyce's mysterious genius. Often captious toward fellow writers, he wrote to George Bernard Shaw when Shaw received the Nobel Prize, saying that it was satisfying to see a fellow Dubliner honored. He would have known that no one before or since deserved it more.

Though having the fragility of a deer or a bird, and dogged by ill health and ill luck, he was as well invincible. George Roberts, his procrastinating publisher who blamed his subsequent downfall on a Joyce curse, compared him to the Giant's

Causeway, that rocky promontory between Ireland and Scotland. Yeats, who barely knew him in Dublin when he was "a pillar of the taverns," saw his incalcitrance and described him "as a soft tiger-cat." Joyce's cruelty never left him and no one bore the brunt of it more than Miss Weaver. The "intestinal grippe" which his secretary, Paul Léon, wrote to her of, boded estrangement. Léon would pass on requests to send issues of this or that to important people, to send a wreath on George Moore's death and to harry her solicitors to release more of her stock. She was never to learn why she was so ruthlessly cut off. There were differences, as she conceded, over her care of Lucia and there was a justifiable anxiety about his "determined extravagance" but she had never intended to annoy him. All she could glean from Léon was that "her shifting attitude to Mr. Joyce both within the family circle and the immediate surroundings was inappropriate." She was bewildered. She begged to know. Mr. Joyce was not in the mood to listen. She wrote again to say that she was trying very hard to understand the fragments of *Work in Progress* and she blamed her slow dull mind for being so dense in her understanding of "the Mookse and the Gripes," Paleolithic or Tardenosian cultures, the prophecies of Saint Malachi or the chants of Zozimus, a blind Irish bard convert to Saint Patrick.

She wanted Mr. Joyce to know that she had not forgotten him and that she would always assist. In return, she was told by Mr. Léon that Mr. Joyce felt only emptiness in his house and in his heart, his daughter gone and the public not prepared to accept his genius. There would come news of another setback for Lucia or the necessity for Mr. Joyce to go to Zurich for an eye operation and any way that Miss Weaver could help would be "a blessing." She always did. She paid for his funeral and did all she could to support Nora and Giorgio who were in a pension in Switzerland and unable to draw any royalties from *Ulysses* during the war. When she donated Joyce's letters to the British Museum, she omitted a few, those few as she said in which talking of Lucia's deterioration and her resentment of her mother, he had shown his wounds and his heartbreak too candidly. She not only loved his work, she recognized the supreme sacrifice that it required from him and those near to him. In the canons of literature, she is rife for beatitude.

Eisenstein, who went to see Joyce in the 1930s to discuss the filming of *Ulysses*, saw a frail figure hidden behind thick glasses, one a window glass, the other a magnifying glass, a shaman in a darkened room. He only became animated when he could talk about *Finnegans Wake*, his "lingerous, langerous book of the dark." Eisenstein came away thinking of it as a "ghost experience," the pair of them like two shadows, barely communicating. But he recognized Joyce as a great man, a man who knew everything as opposed to lesser mortals who feel everything. There was, of course, a distance of thirty years between the Joyce Yeats had observed and the one Eisenstein had visited, but the metamorphosis in Joyce himself was that of centuries rather than years. Although he believed his work from *Dubliners* onward went in a straight line, though the scale of expressiveness and the writing technique rose somewhat steeply, he could not understand why readers were baffled. With customary audacity he said that what the eye brings is nothing, adding, "I have a hundred worlds to create, I am only losing one of them."

To the European intellectuals who were given audience, he would expound as the mood took him. The only great thinker, he insisted, was Aristotle, the others who came after from Kant to Croce merely cultivated the same garden. His distaste for State and government never left him, the State as he said was "concentric and man eccentric." Material victory was the death of spiritual ascendancy. Another noble pronouncement but light-years away from his straints for money from Miss Weaver. He would remind his visitors of the obstacles he had endured over *Ulysses*, of the senseless things that had been said, and then recall the beautiful metaphor of the French critic Valéry Larbaud, who likened it to the stars of the sky whose beauty increases when they are studied for a long time and new stars are discovered. Other times he chose to say nothing. There might be a bout of frigid silence and then, spurred on by an inner impulse, he would recite Flaubert's "Hérodias," enact the "Dance of Salome," with the head of John the Baptist being carried off by two cumbrous schoolchildren.

This unnerving mixture of aloofness and erudition never left him. Jacques Mercanton, a Swiss critic, describes a walk in Lausanne where the Joyce family were holidaying, and being questioned incessantly about the names of the places they passed, the mountains, the vineyards, the lake, with Joyce repeating the words over and over again, to savor their sounds which had replaced sight and touch. At a blessing of the baptism font in Paris one Easter Saturday, the same writer describes him as looking sad and frightened and needing to grip his friend's hand for safety. He went to church on special occasions, both because he liked the singing and because the Catholic liturgy and ritual represented "the oldest mysteries of humanity."

Many describe him with a veneration, a mystic figure sitting in a room with the shutters closed, or in a restaurant, his hand decked with rings, the cane which he always carried between his legs giving him the aspect of a bird hooked upon a branch, predictably discussing the abracadabra of *Finnegans Wake*. To the French critic Louis Gillet, Joyce was a god, a god espoused to men only. Gillet talks of Joyce's affiliation to the male, calling it the axis of his life, a pinnacle in which woman had almost no part and was dethroned from her role as Beatrice. "Eve's daughters," Gillet tells us, were given only walk-on parts, small roles, *figurantes*. For him Joyce's empathy was male, had nothing to do with trifling affairs of the heart or the senses, was a current going from man to man without passing through the intermediary of female entrails. Hard to tally that with lines such as "Touch me. Soft eyes. Soft soft soft hand. I am lonely here. O touch me soon now."

Stuart Gilbert, who was one of Joyce's willing and lauding disciples, gives a rather grudging and caustic picture of the family during their stay at the Hotel Belmont outside Paris. "Mrs. Joyce" was almost as jumpy as her daughter, getting more and more *énervée*, blaming him for the fact that they had no home and that their daughter was ill. Gilbert said their lives were empty because they did not attach themselves to anything except ephemeral things and that they were too self-centered to make friends. Joyce he conceded was a little more human than his wife but his interests were so circumscribed that he cared only for his family and to a lesser extent his country.

The truth is that the Joyce they saw was a fraction of the inner man. No one knew Joyce, only himself, no one could. His imagination was meteoric, his mind ceaseless in the accruing of knowledge, words crackling in his head, images crowding in on him "like the shades at the entrance to the underworld." What he wanted to do was to wrest the secret from life and that could only be done through language because, as he said, the history of people is the history of language. In fact people had become figments and it was enough for him that this or that character lived in his dreams. Even Finn MacCool evolved into shadow. Joyce pored over words and dialect in order to create the new language or rather the old one, the one he believed existed in its pristine purity before tongues were jumbled. From that original tongue he resolved to recreate forty tongues and said that it was quite reasonable to allow two men to speak Chinese and Japanese in the Phoenix Park, because that was the only logical way of expressing "a deep conflict, an irreducible antagonism." Conflict was at the root of Joyce's thrust and not obfuscation as he was accused of. Being almost blind he was, as well as having to feel the words, a Herculean task which sometimes, Lucia noted, reduced him to tears. Artistic truth was sacred to him, that was his religion—the minutest perfection of style, diverse meters, musical notations and a ravishing lyrical pith. To the Polish writer Jan Parandowski he said that perhaps it was madness to grind up words in order to extract their substance, or to graft one on to another to create crossbreeds and unknown variations, to marry sounds which were not usually joined; assembling and dissembling, forever.

Everything he had to say about work and in particular his own work was scrupulous and illuminating. About other things he was as fallible as the next person. His habit of dismissing psychoanalysis and in particular Sigmund Freud—"the tweedledee of Vienna"—is somewhat abritrary. His understanding of psychoanalysis is somewhat ingenuous. A house is a womb and a fire is a phallus! Freud and himself were namesakes and *Finnegans Wake* is surely a journey of the unconscious attempting to be conscious. He liked to interpret dreams but as Richard Ellmann says, they are a hotchpotch of Freud and the Arabian Nights. Nora's dreams show a richness and complexity in glaring contrast to a description of her by the Danish journalist Ole Vinding, "following patiently as a cow."

In one dream, she was in a theater watching a newly discovered play by Shakespeare, Shakespeare was present, there were two ghosts and she feared that Lucia was becoming frightened. In his analysis, Joyce gave himself the leading role even though he had not featured in the dream at all. The ghosts were related to his theory of two ghosts in Hamlet, Hamlet's dead twin, something Nora would not have known as she never got through *Ulysses*. Shakespeare's presence as precursor of Joyce's and Lucia's fear was for the subsequent honors her father would receive and the unrest his genius would create in her mind. In another dream of Nora's an old admirer, the Italian journalist Prezioso, appears weeping and holding *Dubliners* in his hand. Joyce's interpretation was quite simple. His rival, unable to liberate himself in life, had become an ageing and pathetic wooer. In fact it was Joyce who years earlier had encouraged Prezioso in his pursuit of Nora and then harangued the poor man when he found a letter to Nora in which Prezioso said that the "sun shone for her."

His own dreams are vivid but strangely enough seem more like the unconscious trajectory of Kafka than of Joyce. One that he recounted to William Bird hints at an unspeakable crime. He (Joyce) entered a pavilion in which there were sixteen rooms, four to each floor, and his intent is to go from the ground floor into the garden but he is stopped on the threshold as one drop of blood falls. Desperate to get out he tries each of the four floors and each time, on each threshold, a similar drop of blood falls. The onlookers were executioners in brocaded robes and a man with a scimitar. His interpretation of this is somewhat highfalutin. The room represented the twelve signs of the zodiac, the three doors were the Trinity, the criminal was himself, the drops of blood were the five francs he had borrowed the night before from Wyndham Lewis, and the man with the scimitar was his complaining wife the following morning. For a man who paid particular attention to numbers, there is a discrepancy here. There were four doors, which is not the number of the Trinity, and four drops of blood do not easily convert themselves into a five-franc note. Another dream he recounted to the tenor John Sullivan shows him meeting Molly Bloom in a black opera cloak and trying to explain to her her own episode in *Ulysses*. She is unimpressed and dismisses him with "And I have done with you, too, Mr. Joyce."

The same ambiguity prevailed about Ireland. He claimed to hate it, though it is true that his hatred paled in comparison with Nora's. Asked by a visitor about a street in Dublin thirty years after he had left it, he paused, then went on to describe the cobblestones with the sound of the horses' hoofs, the sound of footsteps and their different echoes, then the smells, musty and otherwise, the smell of fresh and dried horse manure, or "horse apples" as the locals called them, the play of light at different times of day. It must have been an agony for Joyce to be separated from the city he loved so and not to be able to walk about it or to walk along the strand with the tide out, lozenges of sand, water lapping and sidling, dim sun-drenched sea. That landscape was the first enthrallment to his young and highly charged being. And he never forgot it, never really left it, regardless of exile—"that sob of turf for to claim his."

There is one thing in Joyce's life which defies belief. Never in all the years since her death did he allude to his mother. It is hard to think that she who had such a lasting influence on him was not mentioned in any of his letters home and not referred to after his father's death or his daughter's breakdown. It is a fierce and determined repudiation. Her death he had described "as a wound on the brain" and elsewhere he spoke of words as being the sea "crashing in on his breaking brain." Mother's words and sea inseparable. Bloom would muse on the womb-state—"before born babe bliss had. Within womb won he worship"—but James Joyce went on to disavow that. At the time of her death he seemed to show no grief and when he first met Nora a few months later he said that his mother had died from his father's ill treatment and his own "cynical frankness of conduct towards her." But it was more complicated than that. His banishment of her was absolute and when she came back in his fiction it was as persecutor. Stephen Hero says, "Thou has suckled me with bitter milk. My moon and my sun though has quenched forever. And thou hast left me alone forever in the dark ways of my bitterness and with the kiss of ashes thou hast kissed my mouth."

He was a tragic man with a staggering genius for whom humor was a weapon. Oliver Gogarty, writing about him in the *Saturday Evening Post*, said that Joyce was a Dante who had lost the key to his own inferno. Joyce had lost none of the keys and none of the words; in truth he excavated them. Michael Lennon, another loyal Irishman and former police magistrate, writing in the *Catholic World* called Joyce's work "excremen-tious" and accused him of opening the sewers of the mind to an intelligentsia saturated with pseudo-Freudianism. *Ulysses* he decreed "not so much pornographic as physically unclean" and Joyce he deemed had been ousted from his pre-eminence as muckraker by D. H. Lawrence. He ended his evaluation with the nauseating sentiment that there might be in Joyce's heart "broken lights of faith" which could be ignited by his blindness and his despair. Then he posed a question. Had Joyce a future? The answer was no. As poet and novelist Joyce would always fail.

Joyce's future is assured. His shade haunts every great writer who has followed him. The essays, treatises, books and seminars abound, but more tellingly and perhaps more viscerally he is still hated. He joked once to Miss Weaver that after the publication of *Ulysses* someone in Paris had said that he was supposed to be a poet but that his chief interest was mattresses. He would joke again.

Bloomsday in Dublin in June 1998 was a fairly lighthearted event with men and women in Edwardian dress prepared to recite some snatches of *Ulysses*, particularly the risky bits, and "chiselers" as he would call them perched on messenger bikes of that period. A mood of gaiety. A foolhardy gentleman posed in the freezing water at Sandycove holding up a copy of *Ulysses*. Kidneys and the innards of beasts were served at several breakfasts and there was no shortage of drink. A typical Dublin savant confided that when a Japanese author read a bit of *Finnegans Wake* in his own tongue it made much more sense than in the mother language. A banner in Dublin Airport declared it Bloomsday and all around the world from sunrise to sunset pieces of the text were read and conveyed on the Internet. Two days later in a letter to the *Irish Times* a gentleman called Mr. Coisdealagh carried on the missionary work of "Let's crucifice Joyce." He said that the resentful barbs toward the Ireland which exported Joyce were all too evident in "his draft writing." Joyce's books were really not his own because he did not correct his drafts which contained grammatical errors and indecipherable gaffes which readers and printers merrily accepted. He would not, I suppose, want to hear that *Ulysses* took seven years of unbroken labor, twenty thousand hours of work, havoc to brain and body, nerves, agitation, fainting fits, numerous eye complaints—glaucoma, iritis, cataract, crystallized cataract, nebula in the pupil, conjunctivitis, torn retina, blood accumulation, abscesses and one-tenth normal vision. That Joyce has risen above so much misunderstanding is surely a testament to those wounded eyes and the Holy Ghost in that ink bottle.

The battle as to who owns James Joyce infiltrates many a Joycean occasion, a claim so proprietary and absurd that it deserves no answer. Genius is singular and Beckett was indeed right when he said that the artist who stakes his life is on his own.

Joyce's finest epitaph came from Nora who, after his death, wrote to her sister, "My poor Jim, he was such a great man."

Departures

IN HIS LAST YEAR he became more morose, with Nora pleading for visitors to leaven things. She complained that he might not exchange three words with her in a day and he countered by asking what is there to say after thirty years of marriage. It was 1940, private and public tragedies coinciding, Paris soon to fall to the Germans and families having to evacuate the city. The Joyce family were also scattered, Lucia in a maison de santé at Ivry, Giorgio estranged from his "hysterical wife" and embattled in trying to have her sent back to New York while also hoping to gain custody of his son.

Joyce saw the full implications and tragic inevitability of the Nazi invasion and he even saw the "defeatism" of nationalist France but his thoughts centered on his distrait daughter and his neglected book. Never having engaged in politics he would not do so now; he had helped some Jewish intellectuals to leave Europe for America but he would anger Nora and other friends with his hypothesis of Hitler's demonic powers as another proof of the ongoing cycles of history which had been the theme of *Finnegans Wake*. "Let us leave the Czechs in peace and occupy ourselves with *Finnegans Wake*," he said and Beckett, who was helping him to collect papers from an apartment, described Joyce sitting at the piano and shouting in a loud voice, "What is the use of this war?"

Nora and he went to St. Gerard-le-Puy, a somewhat stultify-
ing little town where life was very different to the one they had
led in Paris. The good citizens of St.-Gerard saw "a poor old
man" in a long overcoat, an eyepatch and a stick, stones in his
pocket to keep off marauding dogs. When Nora was not with
him he slipped into a bar to down a few Pernods for strength.
By now he was a skeleton.

Sometimes at a gathering, buoyed by drink and the latent
memory of former revels he would sing, but no longer the risqué
"Oh, the Brown and the Yellow Ale!" The songs now, like himself, were quieter as he sang in a restrained interior voice and
as Jacques Mercanton later wrote, "his face illuminated by the
grace of the moment." Friends would join in the chorus of "Ye
Banks and Braes" but these bouts of gaiety were short-lived.
No one could guess his inner torments and anyhow a whole
world was concerned with a more impending catastrophe as
Denmark, Norway, Belgium and the Netherlands fell into German hands.

"I can do anything I like with words," he once said and yet
he was helpless to do that one thing he so desperately wished
for: to make Lucia of sound mind. Hearing that a nearby hotel
would soon be requisitioned as a maison de santé he went and
saw the doctor to secure a place for her. He can hardly have
been assured by the doctor at Ivry who had come to believe that
the night alerts of the air raids could prove beneficial to highly
strung patients. In her violent moments she broke windows, as-
saulted nurses or other patients but her father still believed
that if she were near him there would be deliverance. Without
her and without writing he was stranded. A writer, and especially a great writer, feels both more and less about human
grief, being at once celebrant, witness and victim. If the writing

ceases, or seems to cease, the mind so occupied with the stringing together of words is fallow. There was nothing he admitted but rage and despair in his heart, the rage of a child and the despair of a broken man. It is not singular to Joyce. Tolstoy in his later years renounced his works and peopled his estate with Rasputin-like zealots who split the family. When Tolstoy left his house and walked through the snow, Sonya, who had borne many children and copied *War and Peace* by hand three times, followed but was refused admission to the waiting room where he lay dying. Eugene O'Neill came to see his wife Carlotta as his enemy and moreover his mad enemy. Virginia Woolf put stones in her pocket and one morning drowned herself in the River Ouse in Sussex. Charles Dickens became lonely and morose, marshaling his children against his estranged wife Kate.

Joyce did not leave Nora and in fact became more dependent on her as time went on. Stuart Gilbert describes a scene a year or so earlier, Mrs. Joyce packing in order to go to a hotel, Joyce curled up in a chair, dejected, saying that he could not look after himself, that he must have her, and Nora suggesting that he drown himself. Then the old arguments about drink and money, the money spent on the Irish tenor John Sullivan when his son Giorgio could have done with such patronage. In order to let them thrash things out, Gilbert left the apartment but at Joyce's request phoned at six o'clock to be answered by Nora who said, "I've given in again." Joyce loved his family and insisted that they were all that mattered to him but as he got older he became less attached to the things of this world; they were, as with Anna Livia, "becoming loathed to him." Words had been his mainspring. He told Ole Vinding that while *Finnegans Wake* had been insuperably difficult it had given him immense pleasure and it had for him a "greater reality than any other."

The fulfillment which the work brought was countered with a devouring emptiness. Camus has written of the actor's terror and even more so of the actor's impotence but the barren writer is even more enfeebled. Because of being able to conjure up worlds, to depict emotions so passionately, to make characters as animate as Anna Karenina or Leopold Bloom, the writer seems invincible but is in fact potentially the most stranded of all. The cliff face is the daily port of call. It is ironic that the righteous André Gide who returned his copy of *Ulysses* said after Joyce's death that what he most admired in him, as in Mallarmé and Beethoven and the very rarest of artists, was that the work completes itself with a cliff, the steep face of its genius an enigma to the end.

For the time being there was no question of writing. He still carried his notebooks and jotted down curious words but he had not finished with *Finnegans Wake* because the world had not begun with it. Asked what he would write next he said that it would be short, then mentioned his love of the Greeks and a drama on the revolution of modern Greece. Had he lived to do it, the Liffey would definitely have invaded the "wine dark sea."

Being British citizens, Joyce and Nora were in danger in occupied France and Giorgio was liable to be conscripted. The family decided to move to neutral Switzerland and the undertaking has in it all the bungle and grinding perversity of a Kafka fable. The Swiss authorities were first approached about giving them sanctuary and there followed the usual bureaucratic rigmarole. Joyce was suspected of being a Jew by some clerk who had confused him with the fictional character Leopold Bloom. Then it was a question of money. Joyce's declaration of worldly goods was so modest that they asked for a guarantee of 50,000 francs. A longtime Swiss friend, Paul

Ruggiero, joined with the art critic Dr. Carola Giedion-Welcker to have the figure brought down to 20,000 francs which they themselves secured.

That done, visas had then to be procured from the Vichy government as more influences were exerted. A deputation from the French Academy came to the small town much to the edification of the locals. Eventually visas were stamped on their passports only to find that Nora's and Joyce's had expired. Giorgio bicycled to the office of the American Chargé d'Affaires and somehow persuaded a clerk there to renew the passports even though he did not have the authority. The last "Homeric" venture involved trying to get a gallon of petrol on the black market so that they could be driven to the railway station.

On December 15, 1940, the "Bethlehemites" made their way out with scarcely any money, one suitcase and a nineteen-hour train journey to lead them to safety. Joyce hoped that once he had settled in he could get permission to have Lucia brought from Brittany but within a week the German authorities withdrew her exit permit and all private transport across France was discontinued. There is no last letter from him and no knowing with what stellar words he would have tried to reach her. He was fragile, preoccupied, refusing food though not drink and when Ruggiero accidentally put his hat down on the bed, Joyce jumped and said, "Ruggiero, take that hat off the bed, it means someone will die." That someone would be himself.

"O, Kinch, thou art in peril," the young Stephen Dedalus had said, speaking for the young Joyce of the sexual pitfalls but now it was the worst pitfall of all—extinction. In January, after a small dinner party in the Kronehalle he was seized with stomach cramps and was given morphine injections for the pain. A day later he was brought out on a stretcher, writhing, and in the hospital was diagnosed as having a perforated duodenal ulcer which he had had for years, something Nora had suspected but doctors had put all his troubles down to "nerves."

Just before the operation he spoke to Giorgio of the two constants that had been ogres all his life—the fear of losing his mind and the shortage of money. He had never spoken of death and when once asked about the next life he said that he didn't think much of this one. He was given transfusions of blood from two soldiers of Neuchâtel. The wine of the region had been a favorite of his, one he had named "the true midsummer night's dream." The surgery was successful but the next day he fell into a coma. He had asked that his wife's bed be put next to his but the staff advised mother and son to go home and he died, as his mother had died, on the thirteenth day, a date he had always regarded as being unsuitable for travel.

His funeral in the Fluntern Cemetery was a modest affair, Nora and George, a few friends, two Swiss dignitaries, a tenor Max Meili who sang Monteverdi's "Addio terra, addio cielo." Lord Derwent, a British minister, said Ireland would continue to "enjoy the lasting revenge on England by producing literary masterpieces." Ireland herself was represented only in a green wreath made into the shape of a harp which Nora had chosen. Paul Ruggiero had suggested bringing a priest but Nora said that she couldn't do that to Jim. An elderly man who had been staying in the same pension as the Joyces had tagged along for something to do and kept asking who it was they were burying. "Herr Joyce," the undertaker said. The stray man asked again and was told again. And again.

If he were alive that is something Herr Joyce would write about—gloriously, comically, and with all the sorrow and muddle which pertains to life and death.

Bibliography

In order of author preference:

James Joyce, Richard Ellmann
The Consciousness of Joyce, Richard Ellmann
My Brother's Keeper, Stanislaus Joyce
James Joyce's World, Patricia Hutchins
Joyce's Book of the Dark, John Bishop
Joyce's Cities, Jackson I. Cope
James Joyce and the Question of History, James Fairhall
Joyce's Lives, Bernard McGinley
Portraits of the Artist in Exile, Willard Potts (ed.)
James Joyce and Sexuality, Richard Brown
John Stanislaus Joyce, John Wyse Jackson / Peter Costello
Nora, Brenda Maddox
Samuel Beckett, Deirdre Bair
Reflections on James Joyce, Stuart Gilbert
The Making of Ulysses, Frank Budgen
The Scandal of Ulysses, Bruce Arnold
Conversations with James Joyce, Arthur Power